"A springboard to the freedom of organized living!"
—**Sandra Felton**, Founder of Messies Anonymous

"Many suffer silently in their clutter, feeling alone, embarrassed, and trapped. Kathryn's book is a gift to those who are drowning in "stuff." It is full of sage advice and practical techniques that will lead you down the road to the fullness of life God intended you to have."
—**Barbara Hemphill**, author of *Kiplinger's Taming the Paper Tiger at Home*

"You can have the result you desire: a life that is rich and under control!"
—**Tammy Maltby**, co-host of the four-time-Emmy-nominated television talk show *Aspiring Women* and author of *Lifegiving: Discovering the Secrets to a Beautiful Life*

"People tend to make change when it *feels* good and when change is easy. Porter will convince you it feels good to let go of clutter because she speaks right from the heart of her own experience. And she makes it easy to do with simple advice."
— **Judith Kolberg**, Director, Atlanta Hoarding Task Force

". . . one of the most freeing stories on letting go of physical and emotional clutter. Porter understands the pain and process of how people collect too much stuff and is right there to help you get rid of it in a grace-filled way. Everyone who suspects they might have too much stuff should read this book!"
—**Marcia Ramsland**, The Organizing Pro, Author & Speaker

"It doesn't have to be overwhelming! Kathryn offers practical ideas and steps for putting clutter in its place. A wonderful resource for every home."
—**Kathy Peel**, AOL's Family Coach and author of 18 books

TOO MUCH STUFF
WINNING THE WAR AGAINST CLUTTER

KATHRYN PORTER

BEACON HILL PRESS
OF KANSAS CITY

Copyright 2006, 2012
By Kathryn Porter and Beacon Hill Press of Kansas City
Revised and updated 2012

ISBN 978-0-8341-2831-6

Printed in the
United States of America

Cover Design: Brandon Hill/Tom Shank
Inside Design: Sharon Page

Library of Congress Cataloging-in-Publication Data

Porter, Kathryn, 1971-
   Too much stuff : winning the war against clutter / Kathryn Porter.
      p. cm.
   ISBN 978-0-8341-2831-6 (pbk.)
   1. Christian life. 2. Habit breaking—Religious aspects—Christianity. I. Title.
   BV4598.7.P67 2012
   248.4—dc23

                                                                    2011048745

10 9 8 7 6 5 4 3 2 1

CONTENTS

INTRODUCTION

THE ULTIMATE COST OF CLUTTER

"She was a wonderful person."

"We are really going to miss her at work."

"She was such a good friend."

"I can't believe she's gone."

"She was too young to leave us this soon."

These are just a few comments made by those who knew my mother. Only a few months earlier, I had traveled to New York for a baby shower my mom and sister threw for me. Now, I had returned for Mother's funeral.

"I am so sorry about your mother. How did it happen?" people asked.

The paramedics had to push aside boxes and bags of junk to clear a path so they could fit the stretcher through the house. There was too much stuff.

Boxes, bags, trash, and debris were everywhere, three to four feet high in many places. A narrow pathway carved a trail from the front door to the couch that served as my mother's deathbed.

"Complications of diabetes," I replied. In my heart I knew collecting too much stuff contributed to her early death. But how do you tell someone your mother died, suffocated by a house filled with waist-high clutter?

This was our little secret. We couldn't share our grief, lest others learn the truth.

A Lesson in History

My mother wasn't always that way. When we were young, she kept a messy house, but never so extreme. Back then, only a single layer of clutter decorated the living room floor. Just a few giant piles of laundry lounged on the couches—as well as the recliner, the coffee table, and almost anything else with a flat surface. We didn't have stacks of boxes everywhere—most stayed hidden in my parents' bedroom.

As time passed, bags of gifts and bargains added to the mounds of folded clothes scattered across the house. Every week, my mother brought home a box or bag full of stuff, perhaps thinking no one would notice. She had a reputation as a giving person and was known for her bargain-hunting prowess. A plethora of gift items littered the home along with clearance merchandise that she *might* use someday. Through the years, the piles continued to build up.

The clutter progression peaked with the death of my grandmother. It was no longer just store purchases, but boxes of my grandma's stuff. My mother loved her mother and could not bear to part with her things. Thirty-year-old perfumes that had long ago lost their scent; expired prescription bottles, some with pills in them; old Christmas cards and yellowed stationery; tattered towels and stained tablecloths; even my grandmother's dentures. My mother kept it all.

We tried to help her; we attempted interventions. She stubbornly refused.

Family Ties

The clutter took its toll on my parents' marriage. They seemed unhappy for a long time, but they were in a committed marriage and stayed together. In my mother's last days, my father remained by her side almost the entire time.

My mother loved her children dearly, but I don't think we ever fully felt the depth of her love, undermined as it was by the messiness of our house. Clutter kills. It diminishes—even destroys—relationships.

The mess affected us in different ways. My baby brother was born with a developmental disability. Unclear exactly how the clutter impacted their relationship, I recollect behavioral issues that arose when the house was at its messiest. Still, in his childish innocence, he expressed deep love for our mother.

My younger sister visited or talked with our mom almost every day. They had their share of fights, but she loved our mother fiercely.

My other brother harbored feelings of anger toward Mother. Their relationship became estranged.

I resented her for allowing us to grow up in a home we were ashamed of. But as hard as it was to love her, it was impossible not to love her.

□ □ □

"We've got a code blue! Code blue!"

"What's happening?" my sister Pam yelled as she ran toward the double doors leading to the ICU. She grabbed a nurse walking by. "Is it my mother?"

We were told we could not see her, that the doctors were working on her. The same response they had been giving us all night.

"Oh no!" she sobbed, "It's her! I know it's her! I want to see my mother!"

Pam barreled through the double doors into the ICU, calling for our mother. Hospital staff grabbed her elbows. Her feet and knees dragged on the shiny floor as they escorted her back to us. She begged them to let go, pleading to see our mother. I reached for Pam as she struggled to free herself from their grip.

Crying, she fell toward the floor as I held onto her. She let out another wail, then her body went limp. Helpless and distraught, she collapsed into my arms as she sensed our mother's passing.

□ □ □

Like Mother, Like Daughter

I loved my mom, but I did not want to be like her. I was so proud I wasn't like her. Then I had to sort through her things. There was so much stuff: Payroll checks that had never been cashed; envelopes saved for their return addresses; bins of gift items; lost cash; old purses filled with money and papers; clothing with tags still on.

As I sorted, I began to realize there were some habits I had picked up from her. I had de-cluttered a lot in my own home, but I saw where I was headed if I didn't continue making changes in my behavior.

I lost personal and payroll checks. I saved cards to transfer addresses to my contact list. I bought gifts throughout the year and stored them in bins. I tended to lose money. I often bought a new purse because the task of cleaning out my current one was too daunting. Unworn clothes I planned to wear someday hung in the closet with the price tags still attached.

I am my mother's daughter.

CLEANING WITH DAD

My father and I spent countless hours going through folders, mail, and various papers. Our mourning consisted of sifting through clutter in a quiet, lonely house. Although filled with mountains of stuff, each room felt eerie and empty, devoid of life.

We worked our way through at least fifty large office boxes stuffed with manila envelopes and folders. Each envelope contained varying combinations of coupons, napkins, recipes, and cash. Some envelopes were empty. Others held newspaper articles, unused stamps, or wrappers. Most were stashed with coupons and recipes with an occasional savings bond here and there. We had to check every one because we didn't know which ones might be hiding money.

Over the course of more than a month, we sat in silence each day and opened piles of envelopes, searching for valuables left behind. We found expired coupons dating back more than fifteen years. We discovered savings bonds my mother never told my father about.

Christmas cards written, but never sent. Recipes and directions to craft projects she saved for future use.

The number of coupons and recipes was staggering. I thanked God my sister Pam did not have to experience the mind-numbing effect of glimpsing into this portion of our mother's life.

A couple weeks after I returned to Colorado, I received a phone call with a timid, shaky voice on the other end of the line.

"Kat? You won't believe this. I've been going through a couple boxes Mom left at my house. It was nothing but envelope after envelope full of recipes and coupons."

"I know, Pam."

"You know?" inquired the quivering voice. "Is that what you and Dad were doing all that time?"

THE ULTIMATE COST OF CLUTTER

I believe my mother's love for things contributed to her early death. She collected stuff she thought she could use someday: recipes to bake for us; craft projects to make for us; coupons to save us money; gifts to give us. Yet the best gift she could have given was more time with us. Time we were robbed of—moments of her life that the clutter stole.

Her death certificate listed ketoacidosis as the cause of her death, a condition that can occur when a diabetic does not follow the proper medical care. As the clutter increased, my mother stopped taking her medications. It appeared she tried to take them, but then gave up because they were constantly lost in the clutter. I found numerous prescription bottles in her name among the collections of things stuck here and there throughout the house—some never opened.

In the end, her possessions owned her. They required her constant attention. Physically, she could not keep up with them all. Mentally, it must have been a terrible burden. And for all that effort, much of what she held so dear was donated to the Salvation Army or left in front of the house for trash pick-up.

□ □ □

I rushed from the airport to the hospital, arriving just a couple hours before my mother passed away. I spent most of the time waiting to see her until the doctors finally cleared us for our last visit. The morphine that eased her pain sedated her into unconsciousness. Only her spirit knew of my presence.

Although she could not hear us, we said our goodbyes. The EKG readings slowed to a flat line as her weak, tired body gave up.

She was only 57 years old.

SOMETHING TO THINK ABOUT

- How does clutter impair your lifestyle? Do you lose things? Do you spend extra money buying items you already have? Think of specific examples.
- In what areas do you struggle most in your battle against clutter?
- How would you feel if an unexpected guest knocked on your front door? Would you invite him or her in? Or would you just happen to be on your way out the door and politely excuse yourself? What do you need to do so that you feel comfortable welcoming visitors inside your home?
- How has the too-much-stuff lifestyle affected your relationships? What would you like to change?
- When God calls you home, what kind of earthly living quarters do you want to leave behind?

HOMEBUILDING

"For I know the plans I have for you," declares the LORD, *"plans to prosper you and not to harm you, plans to give you hope and a future."* —Jeremiah 29:11

The bittersweet story of my mother's struggle with clutter does not have to be your story. God has great plans for you. He loves you through all the messes you make in life, and not just the ones involving clutter. He knows you're not perfect, yet still desires a prominent place in your life.

Do not be discouraged. For when God is our hope, we know we have a future.

1 DECLARING WAR AGAINST CLUTTER

FROM my great-grandmother to my mother, I observed each generation accumulate more stuff. My great-grandmother kept a beautiful home, but the clutter hid in the basement, in closets, and in drawers. Everyone battles clutter to some extent—even neat-freaks. Many can relate to my great-grandmother, who kept the visible areas under control so that the rest of the world didn't know the secret. I can tell who these people are in my de-cluttering workshops. Their faces turn red as they try to hold back their snickers.

My grandmother kept a nice home, but the clutter crept into the perimeter of her living areas and expanded into the bedrooms and the garage. A lot of people relate to my gram. She's who I identify with most.

After my grandmother came my mother. Mom's clutter engulfed the entire house, leaving only pathways to travel from one room to another. The laughter turns to silence as I watch a sea of eyes well up with water. I can guess the hoarders. Their tears look different. I see the pain in their faces—a familiar look that I used to see in my mom. Sometimes they share their stories with me.

Whether junk drawers or junk rooms, we all battle clutter. You see, there is always something needing to be cleaned or tossed. Everybody deals with that. Stuff invades our homes on a daily basis. No matter what your battle looks like, I hope my story will help you.

MY STORY

Some people say you are born with it—that ability to be tidy housekeepers. I don't believe that we're born with an innate talent to clean or that there are "neat-freak" and "messy" genes and everyone has one or the other. So where does it all begin? I can only tell you where it started with me.

It's true that children learn more by what is caught than what is taught. Although my parents taught me how to clean, I caught the behaviors that invited clutter. I embraced behaviors such as saving all kinds of stuff and buying more than I needed. I became inclined to stockpile items for future use and place emotional attachments on trivial things. I can also see how some childhood games may have developed into adult habits.

GAMES KIDS PLAY

Consider the baby who likes to play "drop it." You know the game. Baby drops the food or toys on the floor. Mommy (or any adult or sibling) picks it up and gives it back to baby. Tiny hands drop it again for Mommy to pick up. I imagine this was my favorite game as a baby, but I'm not so fond of it now that I'm a mom.

Envision the toddler who enjoys playing "empty it." Little hands explore junk drawers and fling pencils, screws, plastic thing-a-ma-jigs, old mail, and every last piece of whatever is jammed in there. I was that adorable toddler making this not-so-cute mess. And how about those bookshelves? There's no better fun than emptying all those shelves of books, videos, knick-knacks, and décor. My parents' home had a lot of shelves. Need I say more? Oh, and don't forget about the clothes in the laundry basket. Whether the clothes are clean or dirty, what a fun mess-making game. Small hands enjoy testing boundaries with these and other versions of "empty it." (My toddler mastered this game quickly, but it took a little longer to learn "put it back.")

Preschoolers graduate to what I call "leave it." Children this age like to play with their own toys. They make a mess and leave it for someone else to deal with.

My nieces invited me to play this game, but they stopped enjoying it when I changed the rules. I told them that if they care so little about their toys to leave them lying around, then Aunt Katie will throw them out. The astonished looks on their faces were priceless. This may sound mean, but please understand they owned nearly enough playthings to fill a Toys-R-Us store.

As my nieces grew older and still wanted to play "leave it," I took a kinder, gentler approach. I taught them that the more toys they had, the more they had to pick up. I shared that more toys meant more cleaning. Suddenly, they were eager to find toys they no longer loved and donate them to charity. I wish I had been given this lesson when I was a child.

Without setting boundaries on the amount of toys and expectations to pick them up, endearing preschoolers may very well play "leave it" long into their teenage years. Worse yet, this could be ingrained as a character trait that will follow them into adulthood. Combine the lack of boundaries, the proclivity to accumulate more stuff, and failure to teach children to let go of some of the things they already own. That's a recipe for disaster.

A GROWN-UP STRUGGLE

In the past, I left dirty dishes in the sink. More than I would like to admit, I ignored piles of laundry pleading to be washed. If books, boxes, or bags littered the floor, "leave it" was my motto.

But not putting things away was only part of the problem. The older I got, the more stuff I attained. And I seldom parted with any of it.

I had every intention of going through everything and putting it all in order. But there was too much stuff to organize. I was trapped by the behaviors I caught growing up: amassing scads of hobby items, clothing, linens, and dishes; accumulating junk mail, old bills, cards, and coupons; boxing and storing old clutter to make room for the new.

Subsequently, I lacked confidence in my cleaning skills. It wasn't that I didn't know how to wipe down a counter. The problem was that I couldn't find the counter. I knew how to clear the floor to vacuum, but I was clueless about how to keep all that stuff from creeping back.

I didn't want to be like that. I didn't want to live that way. But I didn't know how to change. Why did it appear so easy for others to keep beautiful homes? What was I doing wrong?

Having a presentable home seemed like an impossible dream, yet I knew it was possible because others did it. I read every book I could get my hands on about organizing and cleaning. I enlisted the help of friends and family whenever possible. I tried several different cleaning systems: index cards, timers, charts, incentives, schedules, and just about every other method out there. But for all my efforts, my best achievements were only temporary fixes.

A LITTLE BIT OF PRAYER

Initially, I didn't think about seeking God in my struggle. I thought, *What does God have to do with cleaning a house?* It wasn't as if He would snap His fingers to miraculously transform my messy living quarters into a sparkling, clutter-free home. Sure, I offered some half-hearted prayer attempts. You know the kind, when you're approaching a traffic light while driving to work and you say *Please, Lord, make the light stay green.* But I tried everything else, so I figured it couldn't hurt if I started to seriously pray about it.

I prayed. And prayed. And prayed some more. All the while, the clutter just kept breeding. Then I waited. And continued waiting while praying, wondering why my prayers weren't being answered.

God heard my cry for help with housekeeping skills but responded in His timing. Though He didn't answer me overnight, He did answer me. And it was not the answer I expected.

PERSEVERANCE PAYS OFF

I met Holly and Jan at church. They had reputations for keeping beautiful homes, so I asked for their help. When they came to my house, I saw that it was difficult for them to understand how I could not know how to keep it clean. Holly made a comment about all the clutter. Clutter? What clutter? It was my stuff. And my things just needed a home. The issue was my cleaning and organizing, not my stuff, right?

Wrong.

I decided to take a new approach. These women seemed to know about clutter, so I asked them to teach me as if they were teaching a child. I told them to think of me as a four-year-old who didn't know anything about housekeeping. Somewhat startled by my request, they complied. So there I was, a college-educated professional being taught the fundamentals of cleaning as one would teach a preschooler. I earned a master's degree in special education, and now Jan and Holly were giving me one.

YOU CAN'T KEEP IT ALL!

"You can't keep everything and keep a clean house." Those words, spoken ever-so-casually, changed my life.

Jan helped me clean the bathroom closet. She stared at the shelves packed with soaps, lotions, candles, picture frames, and knick-knacks. "Why are you keeping all this?" she asked.

"A lot of these were gifts. I don't know what to do with them," I said.

"If you are not using them, then why are you keeping them?"

"I don't know. I guess because they were given to me. I can't just throw all these things out. It would be rude. If people found out I threw away their gifts, it might hurt their feelings." I replied to Jan's question, and then wondered if it might be okay to toss away presents.

Continuing to find more unused, unopened items, she gently prodded, "Well, what are you saving all this stuff for?"

"I don't know. I thought I'd find a use for it someday. I might meet someone who could use some of it. Maybe someday I will actually use some of it."

"Well, can we either throw these out or give them to charity? You can't keep everything and keep a clean house."

It was like hearing the magic words. *You can't keep everything and keep a clean house.* I never thought of it that way. These words made my elusive dream suddenly reachable. It was the answer I prayed for.

QUESTIONS, QUESTIONS, AND MORE QUESTIONS

It didn't occur to me that it was permissible to get rid of nice gift items. After all, I watched my great-grandmother, my grandmother, and my mother save everything—including gifts they did not use—along with the boxes, the wrapping paper, the ribbon, and the tissue.

My curiosity took over. What else could I get rid of? How do I decide what to keep? What other things have I been holding on to that I really don't need?

I talked to my friends who kept nice homes. Instead of asking for help with cleaning or organizing, I asked them about their methods of handling clutter. How do they keep their homes free of too much stuff? What do they do with possessions they used to love but have outgrown? What happens to expensive items they no longer use?

I compared my habits to theirs. Do they keep duplicates? How many bath towels do they own? How many sets of sheets do they own for each bed? What about extra blankets? Are there items they stock up on? What types of keepsakes do they save?

I thought about all the clothes stuffed in dresser drawers and crammed in closets. I always had piles of laundry—clean or dirty—because I didn't have enough room for it all.

How many pairs of jeans does one person really need? And what about T-shirts and sweatshirts? Do I need all I have? What don't I wear anymore? Are there clothes that don't fit well or don't suit my figure? What do I have that I just don't like? Am I hanging on to clothes that are torn, faded, or missing buttons? If so, why am I keeping them?

You can't keep everything and keep a clean house. Although this common sense statement is a simple, obvious fact, it was not obvious to me. No matter how many books I read, how many people tried to help me, or how many cleaning strategies I attempted, the clutter was always in the way. I simply had too much stuff. To learn it, I had to hear it: *You can't keep everything and keep a clean house.*

How did I miss realizing that having too much stuff prevented me from having the home I desired? Until Jan and Holly pointed it out to me, I never knew so much of what I pictured as valuable amounted to nothing more than clutter.

ABOUT HOARDING

You've read my story, but there are other stories out there. Different stories. Hoarding stories. You hear about them in the news. You watch them on reality television shows. Perhaps you know someone who has or is living that story. Maybe that's even your story.

Or maybe your situation isn't as extreme as those of the hoarders you've seen on television or in the news. But those stories had their beginnings somewhere. You might be an earlier version of who the hoarders are today.

My mom wasn't always a hoarder. It started out just being messy. If I hadn't made changes in my life, that could have been my story too. Could you be a hoarder or on the road to becoming one? See if you relate to any of the following.

Hoarders feel such strong emotional attachment to things that letting go of their possessions—even things like an old pair of socks with holes—is like amputating a part of themselves. They feel intense pain, even fear.

People who hoard take clutter to a new level. Rooms in their homes no longer function according to their original purposes; they become storage facilities for stuff. In extreme cases, *everything* holds value, including broken toys and open, crusty ketchup packets.

Obsessive compulsive tendencies also play a role in hoarding and the ability to part with clutter. For example, hoarders may insist that items belonging to a set need to be re-united before letting them go. Or they might insist on washing and folding all of the articles of clothing they're willing to give up rather than just putting them in a bag for charity pickup and being done with it. That is, if you can convince them to part with any of it in the first place.

Sometimes there is an Obsessive Compulsive Disorder (OCD) diagnosis and sometimes there's not. Though my mother did not meet the criteria for the OCD diagnosis, she exhibited some OCD characteristics. While going through old shoes with Mom, she agreed to get rid of a bunch of them, but only if they were mated. She refused to place one shoe in the charity box because we couldn't find its mate. She was sure she would find it once she sorted through the other hundred boxes of junk.

What seems irrational to the typical person is reasonable to the hoarder in their justification to keep things. Everything has a use, though little of it gets used.

Hoarders give many reasons for holding on to things. Sometimes they want to keep items for informational purposes or because they like the way it looks. Other times, they refuse to throw stuff away because they don't want to be wasteful. Not bad reasons in and of themselves, but hoarders take this to an extreme.

I remember helping my mom clean. She insisted on keeping stacks of old magazines, even though she'd never have the time to read them all. A stained towel with frayed ends still had life in it. Brand new drapes that sat in storage for decades might get hung someday. Chipped plates could still be used to serve food. Most every time I asked her if we could throw something away, the answer was, "No, I like that." Even broken knickknacks.

Hoarders often refuse to get rid of things such as old papers—it doesn't matter if the content is outdated or if they can access the articles online. They like the way everything looks. They want to be good stewards of every little piece of junk while the conditions of their homes deteriorate.

STUFF VS. RELATIONSHIPS

Hoarding causes rifts in relationships. It's one of the markers for a hoarding disorder. Your spouse and kids don't understand why you have to keep everything, and you don't understand why your family thinks you don't love them. But this is why: when you cling to your possessions, you hoard your heart from others. You bury it in the stuff around you. Loved ones believe the stuff is more important to you than they are. They wish you could love them as much as you love the clutter.

Cluttered Homes, Cluttered Hearts

If you hoard, it might be to cover your own hurting heart. You bury your brokenness in stuff. Your grief is so painful that you cope by surrounding yourself with possessions.

I saw this with my mother. After the unexpected death of her baby brother, whom she saw every day at work, followed by the death of her mother the same year, Mom's fragile heart couldn't take any more pain. What once was just a messy home became a hoard of junk. From inherited items to recent purchases, the clutter took over.

A clean home won't heal a heart in agony, but don't settle for a cluttered home that only numbs the pain. It might not feel like it now, but you can find joy again.

As a Christian, you don't get a free pass from bad things happening. But you do have God with you to get you through them. God won't make you go through the dark times alone. He will give you the people and resources you need.

If you suffer from severe grief or trauma-related depression, seek out a Christian counselor trained in hoarding issues. You might need extra help to deal with the inner clutter in order to make headway on the clutter in your home.

You Are More than Your Stuff

People who hoard—along with their families—often view themselves as organizationally challenged, messy, or lazy. They use terms such as *too busy* or *too tired*, then blame the mess on lack of help from other family members. They deny a problem exists because hoarder sounds like such an ugly, bad word.

But hoarders are not bad people. They have some of the biggest hearts in the world. Who they are is more than the stuff that clutters their homes.

My mother may have missed the mark when it came to housekeeping—as so many of us do in one way or another—but she was a wonderful person. When I was a child, she read to me, did arts and crafts with me, walked me to the park, played cards with me, took me to the beach, and cheered me on at my softball games. Mom made sure my siblings and I received a solid religious foundation. When it came time for IEP meetings for my brother, she did her research, came prepared with advocates, and knew more than most special education teachers. Mother put her life on hold for months as she and her sisters cared for my grandma in her fight against lung cancer. She did it so Gram could spend her final days in the comfort of her own home with loved ones at her side rather than being cared for by strangers in a hospice. Mom loved that much.

You don't have to let a messy home or hoarding disorder define you. There's more to you than the stuff. That's why I encourage you to let go of it.

THE ROAD TO CHANGE

So what about you? Why do you have too much stuff? What's your story? Whatever your answers, there's no judgment here—only grace.

If you hoard, you will probably need more than this book to defeat the clutter. Check the appendix for a list of Web sites you can visit where you can find organizing help, connect with support groups, or get information about seeking treatment. You can also visit my Web site at clutterwise.com for additional resources.

Do you want to make changes in your life? Start with the way you view yourself.

You don't have to wonder if you should call yourself messy, chronically disorganized, or organizationally challenged. You don't have to choose between being messy, being a clutterbug, or being a hoarder. I am giving you a new title. You are a *clutter warrior*. Say it out loud and then say it again. Let me hear you: "I am a *clutter warrior!*"

Whether you struggle with a few junk drawers, a messy home, or a hoard of stuff, it's time to declare war on clutter. And with that, your new story begins today.

SOMETHING TO THINK ABOUT

- Do you still play "drop it" and "leave it"? What childhood habits do you need to change? What behaviors can you replace them with?

- Are you open to paring down any of your collections? What items are you willing to consider letting go?

- Which do you desire more—to keep everything you own or to keep a clean house? How do your behaviors align with your answer?

- How do you feel when de-cluttering items from your home? Do you enjoy letting go of things you no longer use or need? Why is it easy or hard for you?

- If you were to write your story, would it be a hoarding story? If yes, what measures will you take to get help? If no, what supports do you need so that you can keep a presentable home?

HOMEBUILDING

By wisdom a house is built, and through understanding it is established; through knowledge its rooms are filled with rare and beautiful treasures. —Proverbs 24:3-4

The first step in maintaining a clean house is obtaining the wisdom in how to do it. Nearly anyone can keep a clean house for a day. But *every* day is a different matter. We must seek understanding in how to permanently transform our cluttered rooms into blessing rooms.

Consider that the most beautiful treasures filling our homes are not our possessions, but the people who live with us.

2 CLUTTER BOOT CAMP

BEFORE we attack the clutter in our homes, we need to understand the enemy. You are now a clutter warrior, and this is your boot camp. Here, you will receive your basic training in the types of clutter that surround you and the lies you've been fed that can make you a prisoner in your own house.

What is clutter? How do you determine the meaningful stuff from the junk? You will get different answers from different people. What holds value and utility to one person can hold the opposite to another. Early in our marriage, my husband started collecting Hot Wheels Monster Trucks. They were clutter to me, but these miniature monster trucks were of great value to him. As a monster truck enthusiast, he enjoyed the thrill of the hunt to locate every model ever made. Who was right? We both were. (Since then, he sold his collection and found new items to collect.)

However, some things are defined as clutter no matter who you ask. For instance, anyone should tell you that the McDonald's bag with the used burger wrapper sitting on your kitchen table is clutter.

To obtain a deeper understanding, I created expanded definitions for this foe called clutter:

- Trash: Yes, one person's trash can be another person's treasure, but there are some things that are just plain trash.
- Unorganized things: Even valuable items amount to clutter if you can't find them.

- Unfinished projects: These are the projects that you have given up on. If you haven't worked on it in over a year, consider it an unfinished project.
- Homeless things: Good things turn into clutter when they are haphazardly strewn about.
- Unused items: Consider frequency of use as well. You may want to keep the Christmas tree you use every year, but rethink the bicycle you haven't ridden since college.
- Unnecessary duplicates: Do you really need the extra blender?
- Visually displeasing objects: Why keep something if you think it's ugly? But be careful on this one. You may not like your kitchen table, but if it's the only one you have, it's not clutter.
- Broken items: If that coffeemaker doesn't work, then toss it and buy a new one.
- Ill-fitting garments: How long have you been holding on to those jeans in case you can ever squeeze into them again?
- Outdated or obsolete things: Still using a pre-Pentium class computer? If it does the job, then fine. Just be sure you're not using it as a paperweight because you paid $4000 for something that today you can't even give away.
- Too much of anything: Do you really need fifty pairs of socks? The fewer you have, the fewer you have piling up in the dirty clothes hamper!

Did you ever think there could be so many definitions for clutter? Becoming familiar with them makes it easier to say good-bye to our stuffaholic tendencies. To free ourselves from the things that enslave us to extra and unnecessary housework, we first need to recognize these collections around our home for what they are—clutter.

Do a mental inventory on your home. In your mind, walk through each room in your house. What types of clutter do you see? As you read over the following list, think of the items in your home that you can add to each example.

- Paper (junk mail, napkins, books)

- Clothes (items that are outdated, unflattering, stained, or torn)
- Toys (broken, unsafe, old, or unused playthings)
- Gadgets (high maintenance devices, seldom used appliances)
- Kitchenware (excessive pans, chipped dishes, dusty mugs)
- Obsolete technology (old CDs, floppy disks, VHS tapes)
- Food (expired or moldy "tasty" treats)
- Plastics (grocery bags, butter containers)
- Outdoor stuff (weeds, broken lawnmowers, junk car)
- Pet supplies (chewed up collars, cat litter on the floor)
- Decorative items (knickknacks, faded wall hangings, furniture serving no purpose)
- Excess holiday items (gifts, wrapping paper, cards, decorations)
- Grooming supplies (dull razors, perfume that lost its scent, old makeup)
- Inherited things (someone else's stuff passed on to you)

Now, let's take a look at how our actions—the use of our own free will—invite clutter into our lives. Clutter does not walk into our homes by itself. How we behave directly relates to how much stuff we bring through our front doors. Our attitudes and behaviors produce a too-much-stuff lifestyle.

Consider what you welcome into your life and the behaviors you need to change to stop the flow of this insidious enemy.

Sentimental Clutter (items you keep because of emotional attachment to a specific event or season in life)

My mom friends find it especially difficult to toss old baby clothes. It's one thing to keep a few favorite outfits. It's another to keep everything your baby ever wore. My husband threw a fit the first time I tried to throw out his old, shoddy gym shorts from high school. After recognizing he retained mementos of far greater value from that time in his life, he finally agreed to say good-bye to the shorts. I struggled with letting go of cards and letters—until I experienced the joy of de-cluttering. By not holding on so tight to every scribble from the past, I made room to live to the fullest in the present.

Inherited Clutter (anything you keep *only* because it was passed down to you)

When my great-grandfather passed away, my grandmother had trouble throwing away anything with his handwriting on it. She held on to the ugliest mementos just because he owned them. Likewise, my mother kept my grandmother's old hair rollers and useless gadgets. Not everything is an heirloom. We have a choice: we can leave our children with a legacy rich in memories or a legacy defaced by clutter. Let's honor our loved ones who are no longer with us by cherishing their memories rather than enshrining their belongings. Share funny stories. Laugh about the good times. Remember the love.

Vanity Clutter (things you buy to impress your friends, keeping-up-with-the-Joneses purchases, unnecessary luxury items)

When my husband and I bought our first house, I based my definition of necessities on what other people owned. I thought we needed a guest bedroom because almost everyone I knew had one, so we bought a larger home than what we needed. We foolishly embraced higher mortgage payments to buy a bigger house so we could have more space to store stuff. Vanity causes clutter and costs money.

Samaritan Clutter (items you keep to help others someday)

While going through the garage, I asked my husband why he needed so many drills. Why have a cordless drill and one with a cord? Why do we need three of each in varying wattage? He had an answer for everything, but one response blew me away. "Honey, a neighbor might need to borrow a drill someday. I don't want to lend out my good ones." So we are keeping tools that amount to clutter so we can be good neighbors? We finally agreed that it's okay to say no and place boundaries on lending practices. We won't lend out anything we can't afford to replace if someone breaks it or fails to return it. Of course, we want to be good Samaritans by helping others, but that doesn't mean keeping things we truly don't need.

"Just in Case" Clutter (things you keep just in case you ever need them!)

Why did I keep all those clothes from college that no longer fit? So if I lost weight I would have something to wear. Did you do that? And guess why I kept five muffin pans? Someday, I might want to bake muffins—a lot of them.

"OPP" Clutter (other people's property that you either borrowed or are storing upon request)

At one point, my willingness to store things for friends hindered my de-cluttering efforts. When we say no to storing other people's stuff, we say yes to a clean home for us. And the same goes for borrowed items too.

Clearance Clutter (things you buy only because they are on sale or a good deal)

Who doesn't love a good sale? To clutterbugs, bargains, close-outs, flea markets, thrift stores, and yard sales are what bars and taverns are to an alcoholic. Instead of liquor, our drug of choice is *stuff*. Let's minimize visits to places that tempt us to bring home more clutter.

Financial Clutter (taking on debt)

Credit cards. Buy now, pay later. I've read that we spend as much as eighteen percent more money when using plastic. So we buy more stuff we don't need or can't afford, and then get more bills in the mail. What a deal!

□ □ □

Think you know clutter yet? Now you will have a better idea of what to keep and what to toss. It's a long road ahead, but it's exciting and worth the sacrifice of letting go of possessions you once gripped tightly.

But we need to do more than just redefine our views of clutter. We need to change the attitudes that invite clutter to take up permanent residence in our homes.

THE ATTITUDE/BEHAVIOR CONNECTION

Just as an overweight person cannot become thin in twenty-four hours, neither can the overweight house lose all its clutter in a day. Maintaining weight loss and maintaining a presentable home both require a lifestyle change. A person who wants to lose and keep off the weight must replace or modify certain behaviors. Likewise, a person who wants to transform a messy, cluttered home must eliminate the attitudes and habits symptomatic of "stuffitis."

Years ago, crash diets leapt into the forefront of the news. Weight disappeared fast, only to come back with a vengeance. Slimmer for a short time, crash dieters gained more weight than they lost. Our homes face the same scenarios.

Growing up, our house got cleaned for events such as birthdays or holiday dinners. We feverishly cleaned the morning of the parties, quickly preparing for company. I vacuumed before the guests arrived while my mother boxed up the clutter. I remember how she pushed and shoved to get those boxes into the coat closet. It didn't matter to us that our coats hung on the railings of the staircase instead of in the closet, because the house was clean. Or at least it looked that way to us.

But after the guests left, the mess crept back, only to leave us wondering why we couldn't keep a presentable-looking home. This crash cleaning for special occasions didn't work. It only made room in the house for more clutter. With every closet crammed with junk, more stuff piled up on the floor. Whether it is crash dieting or crash cleaning, both involve temporary change and don't lead to long-term success.

A change of attitude is needed. When we adjust our way of thinking, our behaviors follow. Practicing these new behaviors establishes new habits. Only then can we see permanent change and find victory in our battle of the bulging home.

So where do we get our attitudes and habits? Early in my de-cluttering journey, I realized my heritage as a descendant of a family stricken by the Great Depression impacted my battle with too much stuff. Leftover philosophies of the Great Depression, handed down from generation to generation, affected my way of thinking when it came to deciding what to keep. Back then, when items were scant and money was scarcer, it made sense to hold on to things. And my family held on to everything.

My great-grandmother saved the lard from cooked bacon to use as a butter substitute. Fifty years later, she still lived as she did during those hard times, keeping the bacon fat to substitute for cooking oil. She embraced thriftiness. I recall the butter tubs she saved long after she could afford to buy Tupperware. But she actually used those empty dairy containers. They weren't just sitting around in her cupboards for looks.

Today, if we were to save the bacon fat, it wouldn't be for recycling purposes. We'd hold on to the lard as a keepsake. If we collected plastic butter tubs, it would be to fulfill our new motto of "He who dies with the most containers wins!"

Survival was the mindset of those who lived through the Great Depression. They ate everything on their plates because that might be all they'd have for a while. We either waste portions of our super-sized meals or use our bodies as garbage disposals for the excess food we might feel guilty about tossing. It never occurs to us that we pile too much food on our plates—or too much stuff in our dwellings.

In my family, Great Depression philosophies were passed down, but the rationale behind them changed. We went from need to greed. My great-grandparents cherished spending time with friends and family and trusted in the Lord. In the following generations, we focused more attention on material possessions, forming emotional attachments to our stuff as relationships suffered. We began trusting in *things*. So we accumulated more stuff, bought bigger houses, worked more hours to pay for it all, and struggled to keep clean homes.

Where did you get your attitude regarding possessions? Who taught you to keep all those items that steal space in your house and time away from loved ones? Where did you learn what to keep and what to throw away?

Stop assuming that everything you learned about keeping stuff is true. If your home is ever going to lose the weight, you need to educate yourself about the lies you've been told as reasons to hold on to things. Let's explore these fallacies ingrained into us that encourage us to keep too much stuff:

Lie 1: "I might need it someday!"

Fact: By the time you need it, you won't know where to find it. What about all those things you need now that you can't find because all those things for "someday" are in the way? It's time to get rid of it.

Lie 2: "If I throw it away, I will immediately find a use for it."

Fact: This is a poor attempt to disguise the "I might need it someday" excuse. A friend once shared with me this definition of junk: the things you throw out today that you discover you need two days later. Wrong. Junk is junk is junk.

I don't know of anyone who immediately found a use for something after getting rid of it, but I have seen friends exaggerate the definition of *immediately*. Funny how two days later equates to twelve months later. People with this mentality say things like:

- "See! If I hadn't given away that extra coffeemaker last year, I wouldn't have to buy one now!" (Of course, that's because the glass pot has gone missing in all the clutter.)
- "Don't you wish you saved all of Johnny's baby clothes now that you are pregnant again?" (You are nodding in agreement. Johnny is eight years old. You're expecting a girl.)
- "Honey, I told you not to sell your spare set of hand tools in the garage sale. Now, you will have to lend out your good titanium, Craftsman deluxe set. (The garage sale was more than six months ago. And who says you must lend out something just

because you own it? Yes, it's good to share what you own, but be wise in determining what you're willing to lend and to whom.)

- "If I had only saved those _____ (i.e. bell bottoms, parachute pants, acid washed denim, hip huggers, or whatever the fashion) from high school, I wouldn't have to buy any now that they are back in style." You were a skinny teenager then. You are now a pleasantly plump grandma.
- "I should've kept that second set of pots we received for our wedding. I could sure use them now!" (After celebrating your twentieth wedding anniversary, you finally decide to replace the set you've been using these past couple decades.)

People who are overly attached to their stuff can always find a reason they should have kept their dearly departed junk—no matter how long ago they got rid of it.

Lie 3: "I might fit into this again someday." Let's not forget the more official sounding, "I am dieting right now so I will fit into it once I lose the weight."

Fact: So what if you fit into your old clothes again? If that happens, treat yourself to some more up-to-date fashions instead. Let's face it, most of our "skinny" clothes are at least a few years old. (Side note: The only valid reason to keep clothes that don't fit is if you are pregnant *right now* or *recently* gave birth. If your baby is more than a year old, then it's time to chuck your before pregnancy clothes and buy some new ones.)

Lie 4: Ownership is always an asset.

Fact: From a different perspective, ownership is a liability. Everything we own demands time, attention, and money. Things cost money to insure, maintain, and clean.

That which we possess and that which we desire to possess drains mental energy. We think, worry, and dream about these things. When it comes to the stuff we own, protecting it, insuring it, maintaining it, storing it, and cleaning it is always in the back of one's mind. Even if we're not actively thinking about it, it weighs on us, stealing the room in our hearts we once reserved for loved ones and for God.

Our collections of things clutter not only our homes, but also our schedules. We make time for our stuff—to use it, fix it, sort it, clean it, and organize it. We sacrifice relationships so we can spend more hours at work for extra income to buy things that can't love us back.

Lie 5: "It is good to have extra for backup."
Fact: If your toaster breaks, go buy a new one. You won't have to open a brand-new five-year-old toaster that was stored for backup.

Yes, there are times to stock up. Nobody likes to find out the last person in the bathroom used up the final square of toilet paper. But let's be reasonable. Plan in a thoughtful manner what extra items to purchase based on how fast they are used.

Lie 6: "But I can't throw it out! It was a gift!"
Fact: You can throw it out, so do it! Ask yourself if you really love it. If the answer is no, then toss it.

"But it would be rude!" I know; I once thought that way too, but a true gift is given with no strings attached.

Remember, the gift was a token of love. Throwing it out does not mean you are rejecting that person or his or her love for you.

Lie 7: "It might be worth something (now or someday)."
Fact: If you think it is worth something now, research the value. Check the Internet. Call an auctioneer. Go to the library. It's probably costing you more to keep it than what it might be worth. Account for the hidden costs of storing it, cleaning it, maintaining it, and insuring it. Consider the relational price that it bears on your family.

If you think an item might be worth something someday, consider the potential return on investment. Will it cost you more to keep over the years than what you would make from the appreciation value? How does your family feel about you holding on to things you perceive might be valuable in the future? Are you sacrificing relation-ships today because your stuff *might* be worth something tomorrow?

Lie 8: "All I need are some more storage bins."
Fact: Storage bins are not the cure, just a Band-Aid. They address the symptom (junk and clutter needing a home), but not the problem (too much stuff).

I once thought if I could afford to buy more storage bins, I could keep a clean house. I'd have a place to put all the mess. If I had more shelves, my things wouldn't lie around because they'd have homes. If my closets were designed more efficiently, piles of junk wouldn't fester in them.

I remember complaining to my husband about not having enough room in the kitchen for all my kitchenware. He installed eight ad-ditional cabinets and four drawers, three small shelves, and a long counter. This additional counter became a clutter magnet. I stored so much junk in those cabinets, I forgot what I put in them.

The problem was not my storage space. My problem was the ex-cessive amount of food, dishes, party supplies, and miscellaneous kitchenware I wanted to keep. Organizing and storing clutter was not the answer. I needed to cut down on the amount of things I owned and stop purchasing more stuff.

Lie 9: It's sinful or disrespectful to throw out religious trinkets, med-als, pictures, symbols, and so forth.
Fact: Getting rid of religious clutter is permissible. Remember the verse that talks about seeking first the kingdom of God? Well, how can you seek first the kingdom of God while living in a kingdom of clutter?

When my mother passed away, a friend helped with the de-clut-tering. Scapulas and medals were taped to walls, doors, and windows all over the house. Our friend refused to throw this stuff in the gar-bage, fearing God's wrath would come upon her. That's superstition. God won't condemn you for eliminating clutter from your home. Medals and statues are inanimate objects. They're just things.

Do you recall the Bible verse that tells us to store treasures in heaven where thieves cannot steal and moths cannot destroy? Religious paraphernalia is not treasures in heaven.

Religious items in and of themselves do not bring us closer to God. Consider that grandparents who display countless pictures of their grandchildren will not automatically create a close relationship with them from the photo shrine. Time invested with them builds closeness. So it is with God.

You're not disrespecting God when you get rid of the broken crucifixes, cheap medals sent from fundraising campaigns, or undisplayed statues. In essence, you show respect by making room for Him in your home and heart by removing clutter, even the religious kind.

Lie 10: I cannot keep a clean house because (insert excuse here).
Fact: When you want something badly enough, you will find a way to make it happen. I know the excuses because at one time or another, I used them.

- Too busy to clean? Drop some activities.
- Children require your constant attention? Get a babysitter or hire a mother's helper.
- Don't have enough storage space? Let go of some of your possessions.
- Job too mentally or physically draining? Cut back on hours or pursue a new career.
- Never learned how to clean? Find someone to teach you.

As my attitude changed about hanging on to possessions, I stopped placing such tremendous value on clutter and noticed significant improvements that lasted more than a day. It hurt when I first pared down my clutter collection. But after a day's recovery, I was ready to let go of more. Like a good gym workout, I stretched my decluttering muscles and became even stronger the next day. My house lost so much weight that even I felt skinnier.

By embracing a new attitude to clean out the clutter, you make room for countless blessings in your life. Blessings such as improved relationships, increased energy levels, less stress, better health, decreased debt, peace of mind, and a house that is more than just a structure to hold stuff but also a place that feels like home.

SOMETHING TO THINK ABOUT

- What are some new insights you have learned by exploring the definitions of clutter?
- What types of clutter are most prevalent in your home? In your heart? What benefits do you anticipate from de-cluttering?
- Where do you get your ideas about what to keep and why to keep it? What are some of the lies you bought into that prevent you from parting with stuff?
- What mental obstacles make it difficult to let go of things that clutter your home? How can you overcome these obstacles?
- In what ways do you inflate the value of your possessions? What might it be costing you in terms of relationships, a clean home, and money?

HOMEBUILDING

Do not conform any longer to the pattern of this world, but be transformed by the renewing of your mind. Then you will be able to test and approve what God's will is—his good, pleasing and perfect will. —Romans 12:2

Where does the renewing of the mind begin? It starts with asking God in prayer to change your heart. As you transform your way of thinking when it comes to clutter, ask God to transform you.

Read the Bible and study God's Word. Spend time with Him in a quiet corner of your home and pray. Let Him bring change to your life by building a relationship with our Heavenly Father, through Christ, His Son.

3 PLAN YOUR ATTACK

THE arena is our home. Clutter is the adversary. And this is war. It's time to create our battle plans!

So how do you win the war against clutter? It starts with a plan. I recommend putting it in writing.

STEP 1: TAKE INVENTORY

My baby's nursery was hidden somewhere in the bags, boxes, and bins of stuff. With a delivery date just around the corner, I faced some serious cleaning in that room. Not long after, with a precious baby in my arms, cluttered rooms still tugged for my attention.

It seemed with every two steps forward, I took one step back. For each load of laundry I completed, another pile of clothes grew, lurking in an overflowing hamper. When stacks of paper were tossed in the trash, double that amount pummeled my mailbox. I was making progress, but not fast enough. With every victory, a new obstacle appeared in front of me. Every time I got the house clean, something happened—like a clothing sale at the mall or Christmas.

Sure, I recognized that you can't de-clutter in a day, but things were getting out of hand! I needed a game plan. And it started with taking inventory of the attitudes and behaviors that continued to invite clutter into my home.

Does my story sound familiar? Have you also made progress only to see it disappear? To pinpoint the obstacles hampering your progress, take a personal inventory. Which clutter-inducing behaviors do

41

you fall prey to? What attitudes set the stage for new collections to invade your home?

In what ways do you put the needs of others above your goal to de-clutter? Desiring to be a good friend, I seldom said no to the requests of others. If someone wanted a place to store something, our home was open. If people needed a place to stay, we bent over backwards to make room for them.

How do you express love and gratitude? I showed love for friends and family by bestowing large numbers of gifts. Of course, I enjoyed buying and wrapping all the presents, and my husband relished the fact that he didn't have to do anything.

What are your shopping habits? I was addicted to shopping. A trip to the mall was a treasure hunt as I searched for the best bargain on more junk to fill my home.

How do you view books? There's just something special about books, something captivating about owning my own little library. These bound pages of sacred reading—and I am not talking about the Bible here—were like pearls and rare gems that could not be tossed. Never mind that many of these treasures were stored haphazardly in boxes or flung on a bookshelf every which way. (Even with the popularity of e-books, traditional hardbacks and paperbacks still hold special value to me. Viewing a digital format lacks the sensory experience I get from a book in my hand.)

How many clothes do you own? I complained I had nothing to wear even though my closets—and dressers, hampers, and floors— were filled with an abundance of shirts, sweaters, pants, jeans, blazers, skirts, and dresses. Brand new outfits, tags and all, sometimes found their way underneath the dirty clothes pile. There they waited to be worn, wrinkled and undiscovered, as the styles grew obsolete and the seasons changed.

Is your calendar constantly full? Countless activities once erupted from my calendar. I had something scheduled for almost every day—except cleaning.

What are you doing to take care of you? I tended to put the needs of others above my own. I gave my all to those around me and began neglecting myself. I needed to start taking better care of me.

STEP 2: ESTABLISH BOUNDARIES

Think of boundaries as the ground rules for the battle with clutter. They are the lines we draw that guide us as we decide what to keep and what to toss. They are tools for setting behavioral standards for preventing clutter in our homes. Boundaries tell us what is acceptable and unacceptable. Consider the following:

My house is not a storage facility available for public use. As much as I would like to help my friends with storing their stuff, I have too many things of my own to take care of. (Maybe that's why my friends don't have clutter problems—they just store their things in the homes of others.)

My house is not an extended-stay motel. Nor is it a dorm with openings for roommates. It is my family's sanctuary. If friends or family need a place to stay for an indefinite length of time, I decline their request to move in with us—even if it's only temporary and even if they have a compelling reason. My family is my first responsibility. Therefore, I will not allow other people's emotional and physical clutter to reside in my home.

I will not shop for fun, leisure, or to ease emotional pain. If I don't see it, I'm not tempted to buy it. Therefore, I decide to not go to that big sale at my favorite department store. I know I'll probably end up buying something I don't need that will end up cluttering my home. I will shop from lists whenever possible to avoid impulse buys—or should I say impulse clutter? I will also not use shopping as a means to medicate a hurting heart.

I will establish physical boundaries for my possessions. I will keep no more clothes than what fits in the closet. If a friend offers to give me some that don't fit her anymore, I politely decline her offer because I already have enough of my own.

No more books will come into my home than what fits on the bookshelf. When new books come in, old ones must leave. Even if I have not read them.

I will not allow my home to become overrun with toys. My children will have age-appropriate boundaries on how much they are allowed to keep.

I will establish boundaries with people by saying no and building my "no" muscle. I will decline invitations to home parties that sell stuff. If I go, I will not feel pressured to buy something just because I attend.

Should a clerk at a store try to hand me a sales flyer, I will decline. I don't need more papers lining the bottom of my purse. And who knows when I will get around to cleaning that out again?

I will evaluate scheduling new long-term commitments or taking up new hobbies without giving up a different activity. The more activities I am involved in, the less energy I have to devote to my home. The more hobbies I undertake, the more collections of hobby-related items reign in my household. An overloaded schedule causes fatigue and burnout. Therefore, I will seek balance, carefully considering my goals and priorities. When choosing between good and best, I will go for best.

I will create systems to deal with my family's stuff if they leave the cleaning to me. I cannot force others to pick up their clutter, but I can put it in a box for them to sort through so that it's off the floor. If my husband leaves a screwdriver, glue, gloves, and some miscellaneous items on the floor, I can put them back on his workbench. Until my kids learn how to pick up their messes, I can place limits on how many toys they are allowed to have out at the same time.

STEP 3: CLARIFY YOUR VISION

What do you envision your clean home looking like? To help clarify your vision, let's break this into three parts—the look, the feel, and the function.

The Look

Other than clean, how do you want your home to look? What kind of furniture do you want? What types of décor do you find attractive? How will you fill or leave open the space in your home? What do you see in the small but significant details of your home?

After growing up in a house where taking a design risk meant painting the walls off-white, I love experimenting with color. I want my home to look colorful and coordinated with vibrant yet soothing tones. I like simple styles with touches of elegance. Rather than purchasing furniture piecemeal, I prefer a matching set.

I envision a low-maintenance, streamlined design. For me, those small details involve finding easy-to-clean fixtures and décor. For instance, I once thought intricately carved bookshelves were beautiful. Now that I know about the elbow grease required to clean them, this type of furniture has lost its charm. I see the intricate carvings as crevices to snugly hold debris. More dirt, more dust, more clutter. No thanks.

Instead of selecting décor based solely on aesthetics or cost, I ask the following:

- Do I really love it?
- Is it a want or a need?
- Does it fit the theme of the room?
- Is it difficult to clean?
- How costly is it to maintain?
- Is it so trendy that it will be outdated in just a few years?
- Will it attract clutter?

The Feel

What kind of atmosphere do you desire for your home? Think about how your home makes you feel when you walk through the front door. Does it feel like a dog pound? A hospital? A rock concert? A boxing ring? Colors, scents, sounds, communication styles and even our personal values influence the feel of our homes.

45

I want my home to feel like my sanctuary. When I walk through the doorway, I envision a place that emanates serenity—a haven to rest and rejuvenate where I take shelter from the disorder of the outside world. A quiet refuge of happy noise where I experience the love and laughter of family.

After a hard day's work, what do you feel when you step through the door? Warmth and peace? Chaos and tension? Is your home a retreat or just a building you happen to sleep in?

How can we create sanctuaries for our families? Here are a few ideas:

- Limit music to songs with positive messages.
- Venture toward colors—warm and peaceful or cool and soothing—that make you feel happy.
- Burn vanilla- or fruit- scented candles.
- Greet family members with love, encouragement, acceptance, and patience.
- Express appreciation for one another.
- Build an environment of emotional safety by reserving judgment.
- Focus on the good and avoid stewing over faults.
- Provide gentle guidance with humility and respect.
- Pray together.
- And get rid of the clutter.

The Function

What is the purpose of your home? Does it serve only as a place to eat and sleep? What do you want to use your home for?

I once dreamed of having a beautiful home for entertaining guests. Scads of specialty dishes and party supplies sat topped with dust, even on those rare occasions when I hosted a party. I bought extra bedding, towels, and sundries, not to mention the furnishings and decorations, for a cluttered room guests rarely used.

To meet the needs of others, we flexed our schedule and stretched our home. Our house became a storage unit not just for our possessions, but for other people's property as well. Instead of hosting friends for dinner, we entertained their stuff. With helper hearts and poor boundaries, my husband and I lived by an unspoken door-is-always-open philosophy. Friends and family knew they could stay with us any time they needed shelter, preferring the pullout couch over the cluttered guest room.

Our desire to help others took us off track and set us back in our attempts to create a presentable home. Like a runner who leaps off the track to tie someone's shoelace in the bleachers, we sabotaged our efforts in our race to de-clutter.

With no vision for the function of our home, we gave in to competing priorities that put our own family in second place. Then a friend gave me the wise counsel I needed. She told me to decide if I wanted my home for nesting or ministry.

I realized that God wanted me to put my family first. It's not about choosing family to the exclusion of serving others. I can still be a friend without sacrificing my home.

Nesting means the primary function of my home is to nurture family relationships, establish traditions, and make memories. When I chose nesting, I placed priority on building my family and strengthening my marriage, and established new boundaries to reflect that.

A ministry or community service focus, on the other hand, places greater emphasis on helping others. We decided we could still minister to others without using our home to do it. So we closed our doors when it came to allowing friends to stay with us more than a day or two. We stopped offering to store items that didn't belong to us. We established "family hours" dedicated to spending time alone together as a family—away from outside visitors.

Choosing the nesting function for my home also made it easier to de-clutter. I decided what to keep based on functionality rather than on the notion that items might be helpful to somebody else someday. If something didn't enhance my home for the benefit of my family, I felt free to toss it.

STEP 4: ALIGN YOUR DECISIONS WITH YOUR GOALS

Does the way you run your household reflect your desire to de-clutter? Do your decisions align with your goal of attaining a presentable home?

We're often forced to choose between what is good and what is best. When determining the best choice, align your decisions with your desire to de-clutter.

- Want to buy the sweater you've been drooling over? The price may be good, but if you don't need it, it's best not to buy it.

- Interested in scrapbooking? This hobby adds collections of special books, papers, cutters, and other numerous supplies. It's a good thing to organize your pictures. But is it the best decision to start a new time-consuming activity involving buying, organizing, and storing more stuff? Probably not until you pare down what you already own to a reasonable level.

- Thinking about taking a class on something that doesn't require supplies? Consider the time and energy it drains from your ability to de-clutter. Investigate the hidden costs in the activities you say yes to—such as drive time and prep time. When choosing between good and best, the best decisions align with our desire to de-clutter.

What can we say yes to?

- Need proper organizing tools? Go ahead and buy them.

- If you have a multitude of books lying around with no home, say yes to purchasing a new bookshelf.

- Tired of those hard-to-clean blinds? Replace them with some new drapes.

- Interested in a class on financial stewardship? Improving your money management skills helps you to make wiser decisions about spending money, which ultimately brings less clutter and bills into your home.

STEP 5: RECRUIT A SUPPORT TEAM

Do you know anyone willing to help you de-clutter? Invite others to join your team. Whether they assist by shredding papers or keeping you company, inviting friends to join you makes de-cluttering fun, stimulates motivation, and adds accountability.

My friends, Jan and Holly, each possess unique areas of expertise. Jan's motto is "Just throw it out!" She helped me de-junk while teaching me what to keep and what to let go. Holly was my cheerleader, but nonetheless her support was priceless. When others criticized or questioned the items I threw away, Holly applauded my efforts. Her enthusiasm encouraged me to make bolder decisions when it came to ditching the clutter—such as throwing out my six-foot, artificial Christmas tree.

Another friend helped me battle the onslaught of mail I had boxed up to sort through. She handed me a life preserver during the times I felt as if I were drowning in an ocean of papers.

Choose your support team with care. One of my friends gave me a million reasons to keep the junk I was getting rid of—this is not the friend who makes a good de-cluttering companion.

Involve immediate family as part of your support team. They may not care to help you with the cleaning, but maybe they will agree to encourage you by acknowledging your efforts. Initially, my husband groaned at my plea to join the de-cluttering bandwagon. But when I asked him to encourage me, he cheerfully complied. Eventually, he caught the passion to de-clutter on his own, without any nagging from me. Turns out, de-cluttering is so much fun that it's contagious.

STEP 6: SCHEDULE TIMES FOR SELF-CARE

Your body needs time to rest and refuel. All that mental and physical energy spent on cleaning is exhausting. An overworked body requires a break, and a tired spirit needs rest. Take a day off now and then.

God *commands* us to take time to rest. Think about how you can incorporate Sabbath rest into your life.

Take care of yourself and, if necessary, give yourself permission to take a break from the de-cluttering.

STEP 7: DEFINE YOUR ATTACK PLAN

To win the clutter war, both an offense and a defense are necessary. When we are on the offensive, we sort, toss, and organize stuff that we already own. The defensive approach involves taking specific actions to prevent clutter from entering our homes.

The best offense is a good defense. This rings true not just in sports but also with de-cluttering. Here is why: we're already overwhelmed by the amount of stuff in our homes. We finally see some progress, but our efforts become sabotaged by the influx of new papers, clothes, and toys that sneak in the door. That was my experience.

Defense

Get your name off mailing lists. Ever notice all the junk mail creeping into your home? It invaded my home with such vehemence that I swam in it. I got into the habit of setting it aside to open later, but later never came. Piles of junk mail overtook my kitchen counters, but I couldn't toss it all away without checking it first. Occasionally, what looked like junk mail actually had something of value in it—like a refund or a check. So what can we do to prevent all these marketing letters in the first place? Contact the Direct Marketing Association (DMA).

The easiest way to request the DMA remove your name from its list is through their Web site at dmachoice.org.

Get your name on the "no call" list for your state. Telemarketer interruptions steal precious time from our families and suck energy from our days. At best, they are a nuisance. At worst, they convince us to buy whatever they're selling—something we didn't realize we needed until they called to sell it to us.

Start thinking of telemarketers as clutter salespersons. Decide that you will not purchase anything from a telemarketer. Ever. And get your name off their list. Visit the following Web site to register for the national no-call list: donotcall.gov.

Consider making your number off limits as a contact number when friends transition to new homes. Think twice before allowing anyone to use your name as a credit reference—even for family members. If there is one thing worse than a telemarketer calling you, it's a collector looking for your friend or loved one. I learned that the hard way. Protect your friendships by protecting the privacy of your phone number.

Tell credit bureaus to stop selling your information. Did you know that credit bureaus sell your information to bankers and insurers? That's where credit card companies collect data to market "debt" so you can buy more stuff. Sure, they say they are selling you credit, but in reality, they are selling you financial clutter in the form of debt. More monthly statements arrive in the mail requiring payments on an increasing amount of things you probably didn't have the money to buy in the first place. To opt out, visit optoutprescreen.com. You can also opt out by calling 1-888-567-8688.

Consolidate wherever possible. Review your money habits. Can you close or consolidate any bank accounts? What about retirement accounts? Credit cards? Remember, the fewer the monthly statements, the less paperwork you have to file.

Attrition activities. List and review your activities. Which ones encourage purchasing more materials? What hobbies add to your paperwork? Can you drop any? Even if the paperwork and other related materials are minimal, reducing activities gives you extra time for yourself and more time to devote to home and family.

Offense

Let's take the offensive. Take a proactive stance against clutter. Set the pace and lead others by example.

Don't wait for someone else to clean with you. Stop being a by-stander. Don't tolerate the mess. Step up to the plate, even if other family members don't share your desire to de-clutter, much less cheer you on. Decide to focus on *your* mess without putting the blame on others for the condition of the house. Taking offense means taking responsibility.

Tackle the visible clutter first. Then focus on the "invisible" collections of stuff hiding in drawers, cabinets, and totes. Clearing off your kitchen countertop takes precedence over the junk drawer under the counter.

Think about the rooms you use most and start there. Save the least-used rooms for last.

YOUR DE-CLUTTERING ARSENAL

We must arm ourselves with the proper tools. What kinds of things do you think would be helpful in attacking the clutter in your home? Storage bins? Extra shelving? Closet organizers? Be careful. If not used correctly, these handy tools transform into clutter keepers.

Cool organizing gadgets and extra storage space are not the answer. That amounts to bringing swords to a gunfight. Instead of storage bins, think trash bags. It's time to stop storing the clutter and start eliminating it.

WEAPONS OF MASS DE-CLUTTERING

Trash bags are the major assault weapon in the war against clutter. When you toss personal items for donation, use black trash bags. You might be tempted to keep something you see in a clear bag. Purchase the heavy-duty kind for major de-cluttering sessions. There's nothing that makes you want to quit for the day like watching all the trash you collected fall through the bottom of the bag.

Wastebaskets should be where your family will actually use them. If a certain area is a natural trash zone, then work with it by placing a wastebasket in the vicinity. Make throwing away trash convenient and accessible by placing receptacles in places near the hot spots where refuse accumulates. When we give our trash a home, we won't find it scattered about. Wastebaskets—they're not just for kitchens and bathrooms anymore.

Boxes are necessary for sorting extreme clutter. Use them to put "friends" together. When you know exactly how much you have, you make informed decisions on what to keep.

Don't waste time going to the grocery store for the freebie boxes. Visit an office supply shop and ask for bankers' boxes. Moving boxes also work well. Using boxes that are all the same size and shape encourages organization. Plus, they're easier to store during long-term de-cluttering jobs. Use them for trash or donations as you clear them out.

GRIME FIGHTERS

Not sure of what cleaning supplies you absolutely need? With so many cleansers sold on the market, who can keep track of which ones to use for what? Just as we obtain an excess of clothes, food, toys, and other material items, we accumulate a slew of cleaning supplies. We add to our clutter by purchasing different brands of various types of cleaning agents that perform the same function. Our grime fighting weapons turn into the very thing we battle in the first place—clutter.

My friend Jan, who started me on my de-cluttering journey, also helped me compile a list of cleaning supplies. Jan's secret is simplifying. For instance, instead of buying furniture polish that builds up over time, she dusts her wood furniture with a wet paper towel.

I modified Jan's list for my own home as I discovered sensitivities to the harsh chemicals in many cleaners. Evaluate the grime fighters stocked in your arsenal. Observe how fast you go through them so you do not stockpile too much or get caught with too little. Here's my list to get you started:

- *Rubber gloves*: There are some things you just can't clean without.
- *Sponges*: Throw used sponges out at the end of the day. They absorb more than water. They pick up germs and bacteria that

quickly multiply in this cozy, moist home. These are great for de-cluttering jobs, but I prefer not to use them on a daily basis. Dish towels do the job just as well for daily cleaning and are kinder to the environment.

- *Rags or dish towels*: Washcloths and special cleaning rags fall under this category. Use what you like, but pull out a fresh one each day.
- *Soap*: Castile soap is the one to buy. It's multi-purpose so you can use it in place of your dish soap, window cleaner, and multi-purpose cleaning agents. It cleans floors, countertops, glass, and just about anything. Some people even use it for body wash and shampoo. Most health food stores carry this product.
- *Squeegee*: These are what you see at gas stations to clean windshields. They make them for home cleaning now too. Use them on shower doors and glass surfaces.
- *Toothbrush*: A must-have for cleaning hard to reach crevices.
- *Paper towels*: Whatever brand is on sale will work fine.
- *Chlorine bleach*: I use it mostly for laundry, but I also use it to disinfect the bathroom. When using bleach for tough cleaning jobs, remember to open windows for some fresh air.
- *Baking soda*: I use it mainly for neutralizing strong odors and as a natural powder abrasive.
- *Vinegar*: Vinegar has natural anti-bacterial properties—it makes a good bleach alternative for everyday cleaning. Use white, distilled vinegar for cleaning and disinfecting. Use it straight or dilute it with water. Check online for recipes.

So what about the dish soaps, all-purpose cleaners, bleach cleansers, powder abrasives, bathroom cleansers, and air disinfectant and deodorizers? You really don't need them if you have castile soap, bleach, vinegar, and baking soda. You can go online to find recipes for making all sorts of cleansers with vinegar as well as baking soda.

Instead of using air disinfectants and deodorizers, I open the windows. Even if it's the coldest day in winter, I let fresh air in. For a natural alternative, essential oils and a diffuser work well too. Plus, many essential oils have disinfectant properties. You can also dilute a few drops of peppermint oil with some water in a spray bottle. Peppermint is well known for its antibacterial properties, and the scent is much more pleasant than what you can buy at the store.

If you are not ready to part with your traditional cleaning products, that's okay. Although castile soap does the job on dishes, it's hard for me to get out of the habit of buying the degreasing dish soap. Other agents still make their way into the home if my husband does the shopping. Some messes require specialized commercial cleaners. But as we de-clutter our homes, we can de-clutter our cleaning supplies and simplify our cleaning routines.

Think about keeping a cleaning caddy in rooms such as the kitchen and bathroom, because these are places that demand constant attention. Fill a plastic caddy with your favorite supplies and store it in an inconspicuous place in those high-maintenance rooms. At a minimum, keep a spray bottle of diluted castile soap cleaner, a toothbrush, and paper towels in this mini-arsenal.

STORING GRIME FIGHTERS

Where do you store your cleaning supplies? Do you keep them in the dark recesses under the kitchen sink? That's what I used to do. Canisters got pushed back. Spray bottles spilled. Trash bags ripped. Leaky pipes under the kitchen sink created a sticky coating on items stored there. I didn't care to bring out the cleaning supplies when the counters needed a good wipe-down because it was hard on my back. Nor did I want to pull everything out just to find the one item stashed the farthest away.

Have you ever noticed how businesses store their cleaning supplies? They keep a janitorial closet. Items are easy to find and easy to reach. If you don't have a closet, do you have a cabinet, or maybe an armoire you can convert into a cleaning and de-cluttering supply arsenal? Find a place to keep these items that is convenient. It must be easily accessible so you can grab supplies when you need them.

I cleared out two kitchen cabinets and dedicated that area to store cleaning items. When I began storing my grime fighting weapons in this convenient spot, I grew more inclined to use them. Today, things get cleaned more quickly and more frequently. I know exactly where to find every item, and it's not such a bother to get out the supplies.

Be selective on where you keep larger items such as brooms and mops. Avoid storing them in the entryway. That's where Gram kept hers. A mop propped in the corner and the scent of cleaning supplies just don't say "welcome" the way the aroma of a vanilla candle and a cleared entryway do.

A word of caution: Beware of the "yuckies" ready to besiege you when moving anything that hasn't been touched in a long time. Spiderwebs, dead bugs, and even critter feces may await you. What kind of critters? Let's put it this way. The term *packrat* was not invented because it kind of rhymes or sounds cute. Clutter attracts rodents. Rats and mice make their homes in places filled with lots of stuff. Clutter makes great nesting material. If you come across this, you will be thankful for arming yourself with the necessary weapons.

SOMETHING TO THINK ABOUT

- What boundaries do you need to establish with people and possessions? How can you enforce these boundaries when someone is unwilling to take no for an answer or tries to make you feel guilty about getting rid of your things?
- How do you desire your home to look, feel, and function? What are you willing to give up in order to achieve this?
- Who would make good members of your de-cluttering support team? List individuals along with their areas of expertise. Invite them to join your team.
- What is your defensive plan? What will you do this week to prevent additional clutter from entering your home?
- What is your offensive plan? What weapons do you already have? What weapons do you need? In what room will you start?

HOMEBUILDING

For though we live in the world, we do not wage war as the world does. The weapons we fight with are not the weapons of the world. On the contrary, they have divine power to demolish strongholds.
—2 Corinthians 10:3-4

Another word for stronghold is addiction. All the storage bins and trash bags in the world cannot mask our addiction to stuff.

What is at the root of your addiction? Do you surround yourself with stuff because your heart stings from rejection, sexual or physical assault, emotional abuse, or anything else? Does insecurity cause you to think you need things "just in case"? Were you fed a diet of too much stuff as child, ignorant of the addictive qualities of material possessions? Or is it plain old greed?

Possession overload is often a heart problem. Seek God to heal your broken heart, pray for wisdom, and ask Him to help you do battle with past hurts.

4 BATTLE OF THE BULGING HOME

THE battle plan is drawn. Our drive to de-clutter causes even our family members to run for cover. It's time to attack the clutter.

Not sure where to start? Let's begin with the bathroom and kitchen. If no other rooms in your house are clean, at least get reasonably clear the rooms where you cook your food and clean yourself.

Next, move to your bedroom. This is usually the first room we see every morning and the last room we see before we go to sleep. Most of us spend one-third of the day in the bedroom, assuming we get a full eight hours of sleep. Many spend additional time in the bedroom primping, reading, watching television, chatting on the phone, playing on the computer, or continuously pressing the snooze button on the alarm clock. This is the room where we dream about the future, think about what we value, reflect on life, and rejuvenate our bodies and minds before facing the next day.

You will sleep much better without the clutter. Even though you can't see the mounds of stuff on your bedroom floor once you turn off the lights—you know it's there. You feel its presence around you. And you know the disheartening clutter will be the first thing you see when you open your eyes. Make the bedroom a priority.

Finally, tackle common areas: the living room, dining room, den, play area, office, and other rooms needing attention. Again, start with the rooms you use the most.

Consider your unique situation. If you are getting audited and know your old tax forms are somewhere in the spare room, then perhaps you better start there.

No matter what room you clean first, successful de-cluttering tends to follow a pattern. Generally, a good rule to follow is Only Handle It Once (OHIO). However, severely cluttered rooms call for a more intense battle plan. When you're in the trenches, it is not always easy to let things go the first time we encounter them. Sometimes it takes multiple passes.

THE FIRST PASS: TOSS TRASH

Find the garbage and toss it in the trash. Sell or donate things in decent condition that you know you don't want. If you have doubts about what to do with some items, set them aside to decide later. If selling or donating unwanted items means they will be sticking around for much over a week, don't hesitate to put them in the trash. Your priority is eliminating the clutter. You can't be an environmentalist when you are drowning in stuff.

THE SECOND PASS: GROUP FRIENDS

Ever hear that birds of a feather flock together? Well, find items that are friends and put them together. All photographs in one box. All paperwork in another. Continue to separate belongings into categories. Christmas decorations, stationery, computer supplies, books, and so forth. Toss whatever you can whenever you can. Don't get bogged down with evaluating every single thing. Keep the focus on putting like items together.

THE THIRD PASS AND ON: SORT AND ORGANIZE

Once belongings are grouped together, they need to find a home or leave your home. This is the time to sort and organize the individual papers, trinkets, clothes, and other items.

CLEAR AND CLEAN

After you clear a surface, immediately clean it. You will probably find a layer of grime on those shelves, cabinets, counters and whatever surfaces hold your stuff after removing all the junk perched on them for so long.

Dirty, cluttered counters attract more clutter and subconsciously tell us that it doesn't matter what we place on them. Sparkling counters cry out for us to put items back where they belong. They beg us to preserve their good looks.

Clean from the top down. Floors should be last, but don't be afraid to sweep up those Cheerios on the floor so you don't have a bigger mess to tackle later. Get a regular-size broom for large areas and a hand-sized broom for easy clean-up of smaller messes. Select a broom with nylon bristles. Straw brooms shed, causing faster wear and tear. Plus, who wants the extra work of sweeping up the shed bristles?

A Swiffer is an option that many people find easier than a mop and may be something you want to try.

A quick word on vacuums—steer clear of the kind that need to be assembled for each use or that require you to fill a basin of water. These might be okay for a super-clean, but stick with a low-maintenance-style vacuum for everyday use. A vacuum with parts to assemble with each use only motivated me to find something else to do. I dreaded preparing the vacuum for use more than I dreaded the vacuuming itself. One that just plugs in and switches on is much more appealing for getting the job done, not to mention kinder to your pocketbook.

For small messes, get a cordless handheld vac. These work great for quick clean-up of spills. Keep it in a storage area by the entryway for easy access during the months when mud is likely to get tracked inside.

If you own a multi-level home, consider purchasing a vacuum for each level. I don't know about you, but I get enough of a workout from cleaning without hauling a vacuum up and down the stairs. Think about arming each floor with a broom and mop as well.

KITCHEN STRATEGY

Travel back in time for a moment to visit my messy kitchen. See the piles of dirty dishes in the sink, pots and pans heaped on the stove, and a stuffed refrigerator with magnets and papers covering the door. Look at the mail scattered across countertops and groceries set out in the open while the pantry overflows with food.

Take a good look around. What else do you see? Disorganized cabinets complement overstuffed junk drawers. The hodgepodge of decorations and kitchen supplies piled to the ceiling on the upper cabinets hide the wall behind them. Notice a sticky linoleum floor with pockets of debris under the table.

Let's step back into the present day, but now we're standing in your kitchen. Maybe yours is neater, or maybe it isn't. But regardless of the caliber of mess, we'll begin at the same starting point.

Begin with the Trash

Is your trash receptacle full? Then take out the trash and replace it with a new trash bag. Fill it with whatever trash you find, but don't overstuff it. Look around for things such as junk mail, empty cartons, ratty sponges, and old food. Shred papers with personal information printed on them before sending them to the trash.

Clear Flat Surfaces

What is stacked on your counters and tabletop? If mail, receipts, invoices, and other papers float in your kitchen, grab an office box and pile them all together. Set aside current bills to avoid late fees and disruption in services. If you have a functional paper-handling center, then file items that need to be saved. If you don't have any type of paper organization system, do your best to sort through the box. Keep only what is necessary. You will learn what is okay to toss as you create a filing system that works for you.

Put away items that don't belong in the kitchen. Send run-away toys home to the toy chest. Jackets go back in the coat closet. Return books to the bookshelf.

Check your upper cabinet tops. Are they serving as storage shelves? Grease and moisture from cooking settle in this area, coating stuff with an oily film. Dispose of items not valued enough to keep in a clean place and find safe homes for the valuables.

Attack the Dishes

Start with the piles of dishes in the kitchen sink. While you're there, determine which dishes you really need. Are there any you can live without? This is a great time to toss them.

How dirty are your dishes? Do you find plates with thick layers of mold-encrusted food sticking to them? If it's so disgusting that you don't want to clean it, would it matter if you pitched it? New dishes aren't that expensive. I've seen full sets at discount stores for as little as $20. If your dinnerware is ugly, scratched, spaghetti stained, or otherwise unattractive, go ahead and treat yourself to a new set. Just remember to throw out the old set.

How many sets of dishes and silverware do you own? When was the last time you used them all? Sure, keep extra for entertaining company, but be reasonable. My cupboards used to overflow with dishes. It somehow seemed wrong to get rid of them, but once I pared them down to serve our family plus a few extras for guests, it made cleaning and organizing a lot easier.

After slimming down my dinnerware, I still had beautiful stoneware dishes collecting dust in the unopened box they came in. My husband insisted on saving them, tucked away in a closet because they were too good for us to use. He wanted me to promise to use them only on special occasions. I finally persuaded him to open the good set of dishes by pointing out that using only the ugly ones sends a bad message. Refusing to use the nice stuff communicates a lack of respect for ourselves—that we are not worthy of anything other than second best. Furthermore, I reminded him that every day is a special occasion. Once each day is gone, we don't get it back again. Please, don't let your nice dishes sit in the back of a cabinet or closet. Use them or lose them, even if it's just once a week for Sunday dinner.

Pots and Pans

Now this is an interesting topic. Growing up, my family owned so many pots and pans we stored some in the basement. Learn your cooking style to find the number and types of cookware right for you. What ones don't you use? What would happen if you got rid of them? Do you have another pan that could do the same job?

And while we're on the subject, let's talk storage. I highly recommend a pot rack. It's so nice to have just what you need hanging right there where it's handy. Whatever you do, please, do not store your pots and pans in the oven. It only makes more work for you when you want to use the oven. Imagine preheating your oven filled with pans you forgot to take out and having to wait until the pans cool enough to remove them. Think how nice it would be to open the oven door without having to de-clutter the inside of your oven every time you use it.

How many cake pans, bread pans, muffin tins, potato mashers, egg whisks, cheese graters, and other fancy cooking supplies do you own? Be honest. When was the last time you used some of these? Take a potato masher. I didn't even know this device existed until I received one in a set of cooking supplies as a wedding gift. But once I owned it, I couldn't get rid of it. I might want to make mashed potatoes with it, though I somehow made due without it in the past. And why did I insist on keeping an egg whisk when I always use a fork to stir my eggs?

What else clutters kitchens? Storage containers. Funny how we buy them with matching lids, but then the lids seem to disappear. They're like socks without mates. What kinds of plastic and glass storage containers lurk in your cupboards? How many do you use in any given week? You can pare that collection down. When I de-cluttered my kitchen, I found Pyrex dishes with matching tops. They sure beat the plastic containers. I cook with them and store leftovers in them. Multi-purpose is a good thing. Plastic bags with zipper-like enclosures also store food just as well as the containers. The nice thing about those bags is you can throw them out after you use them.

Ask yourself the following questions with each piece of kitchenware:

- Do I really need it?
- How frequently do I use it?
- Is it easy to clean?
- Do I own another tool that performs the same job?
- Is it broken, chipped, or peeling?

Evaluate the cost of keeping each item. The more you keep, the more you have to clean.

Clean the Refrigerator and Other Appliances

How many magnets cling to your refrigerator door? Can you even see the color of the fridge beneath the clutter of pictures, calendars, recipes, and whatever else finds its way there? Something as simple as removing the magnets (and everything affixed to the door by magnets) gives the illusion of a cleaner, larger kitchen. Minimizing the amount of vertical clutter also makes it easier to clean. Next time you want to wipe down the door, you won't have tons of stuff to take down and put back.

When you open the refrigerator, are you afraid packages will come tumbling out? A little overstuffed, are we? My fridge used to be like that, but not anymore. I don't understand how I ever functioned in the kitchen not knowing what forgotten items were stowed away in the back corners of the freezer. I wonder how I survived grabbing one item from the bottom while worrying about everything on the top falling down. It amazes me how much money I wasted buying food that was never eaten and left to spoil.

Here's the deal on the refrigerator. Because I only go grocery shopping once a week, things don't build up. I actually use what I buy. Food seldom goes bad. At the end of the week, when things look a little sparse, it makes for easy cleaning of the refrigerator shelves. We may not see lots of food when we open the fridge or cabinets, but we don't go hungry. We waste less food and save more money. What a delightful surprise to see the positive impact this new habit made on our budget. Try it, maybe it will work for you too.

Today, I get comments like, "Don't you ever buy food?" and "I can't believe your fridge is so bare!" But I ignore these remarks. I always seem to have more than enough for my family. And it's so nice to reach into my freezer, effortlessly grab what I need, and close the door without causing an avalanche of tumbling food items.

What about other appliances? Anything you can let go of? If you have a toaster and a toaster oven, do you need both? If you can't remember when you last used the waffle iron, must you keep it? Whether it's dishes, food, or appliances, we can't keep everything and keep a clean kitchen.

As you de-clutter, clean. Take a good look at the stove. Is there a buildup of black, crusty, burned-on food on the burner plates? Give yourself a break and buy new ones. Remember, dirt is clutter too. Pull off the knobs on the stove and run them through the dishwasher every now and then.

With all the cleaning products available, what one is best for the stove? That depends on the amount of dirt and mess at home on your range. For reasonably clean appliances, use a vinegar and water mix or any all-purpose cleanser. Castile soap or a degreasing dish soap and a green scrubbie work better for especially hard jobs.

Clean appliances such as the microwave, blender, crock pot, bread maker, and any others screaming for attention.

Thin Out the Pantry

I never claimed to be Betty Crocker. That's why I bought her cake mixes until forced to eliminate gluten from my diet. I remember my mom's cupboard filled with all kinds of Betty Crocker products. If ever confronted with a brownie shortage, there'd be plenty at our house. My parents always kept the food shelves stocked. Duplicates and triplicates of spices and condiments overwhelmed our cupboards. We had enough canned goods to fill a small convenience store.

So how much stuff do you buy for your pantry? I followed the buying habits of my parents, purchasing whatever was on sale, and stocking up on tons of extras—even if I didn't particularly like the items. Today, I buy only what I will need for the week. I keep a few extra staples on hand, but not to excess. Like ketchup. I must have my beloved brand of ketchup, but I only keep one for backup rather than, say—ten!

As you de-clutter your food items, take everything out of your cabinets. Throw away everything past its expiration date. Consider tossing anything close to its expiration date unlikely to be used before it expires. Is there anything you don't particularly like? Then why keep it? Toss anything that disagrees with your palate. Give unexpired items to charity.

Be intentional about which cabinets you select for storing dishes, food, and cleaning supplies. Place dishes in the cabinets closest to the dishwasher. Canned goods and food items go near the stove. Arrange your kitchen in a way that makes sense to you.

One last tidbit on cupboards. What's in the cabinet below your kitchen sink? I challenge you to completely clear it out. Are there things you forgot about? Any cleaners with funny rings or odors? How about runaway garbage? One of the best decisions in helping me keep a clean kitchen was to stop storing stuff under the sink.

Clean the Floor

Technically, this could fall under de-cluttering flat surfaces, but we still want to do the floors last. Rule of thumb says to start at the top and work your way to the bottom. Any crumbs that fell while wiping the table get cleaned up at the end. The same goes for small pieces of paper, food packaging, and dust from items that sat like statues time forgot.

Sweep up the big stuff first and then go around with a broom a second time for the rest. For extremely dirty floors, I recommend getting down on your knees and washing it by hand. Clean sticky spots with a warm, wet washcloth and dish soap. Do the same when supercleaning around the baseboards.

Try to maintain the floor as best you can while de-cluttering. You may not finish the kitchen in one day, but a quick sweep when something drops or spills will make the floor job a lot easier when you're ready to give it a detailed cleaning.

Give Your Entire Kitchen the Eye

Inspect your work. Did you miss anything? Evaluate your organizing. What works? What doesn't work? What do you want to change?

In my kitchen, we no longer pile plates in cabinets as high as the shelves will reach or place different size bowls on top of each other. It makes it easy to get what we need without the trouble of taking the whole stack out to get a particular size plate or bowl near the bottom. We also removed one of the refrigerator shelves. I found one less shelf made more room for storing food. With the extra space, I could store taller bottles upright and have easier access to the smaller items.

Plan on experimenting to see which organizing systems work best for you. Investigate what motivates you to stay on top of things. Learn the strategies and products that make cleaning easiest for you.

Rome wasn't built in a day. And neither was the mess in your kitchen. Anticipate that it may take more time than expected to create the desired look. All the clutter built up over the years takes more than a weekend to sort and organize

BATHROOM STRATEGY

Forgive me if I sound sexist, but I believe that toilet cleaning is a man's job. Come to think of it, that goes for the rest of the bathroom too. My husband vehemently disagrees, so we share the task of bathroom cleaning.

Unfortunately, there will be times when you have to perform this stinky chore entirely on your own. Like, if you're not married or you have a husband who leaves this job to you. Yes, maybe you can hire a cleaning lady, but not everyone has that option.

So where do we start? With picking up the clutter, of course.

Pick Up the Trash

What kind of debris sits on the floor, in the tub, and on the sink? Look for empty shampoo bottles, toilet paper rolls, clothes tags, old makeup, dull razors and any other obvious signs of garbage.

Send Displaced Items Home

Scan the area for items that don't belong in the bathroom. Check for dirty clothes and used towels. Can't see the floor because of dirty clothes pretending to be bathroom mats? Pick them up, put them in a basket, and take the basket to the laundry room. Get a load started while you finish cleaning the bathroom.

If the tub area is a hot zone for dirty clothes, keep a hamper nearby. Think of the hamper as their home until they get washed.

Notice any bath toys? Are children's playthings overrunning the floor? Find a safe home for them. The bathroom floor is not a sanitary place for toys. Some people sprinkle when they tinkle, and you don't want little hands playing with that. Also, beware of backsplash. Flushing causes microbial fecal matter to swirl in the air. The bathroom floor is no place for toys or clothes.

Clean the Sink

What items are making a mess on the bathroom counter and sink? Common culprits found in the basin area include whisker shavings, hardened toothpaste, and soap slivers. If soap rings are a problem, start using liquid soap. Soap in a dispenser tends to leave less mess than bar soap. If your loving husband leaves shavings, buy some disinfectant wipes and ask him to wipe the sink area when he finishes grooming. In fact, leave the wipes out for everyone in your household. Make wipes available for easy cleaning of toothpaste, soap scum, makeup dust, fallen hair, and anything else. When the cleaning supplies are accessible, the cleaning is more likely to get done.

What does the faucet area look like? Befuddled by the gunk around the sink fixtures, I despaired at ever getting my bathroom totally clean. Then I read somewhere to use a discarded toothbrush for these areas.

Clean the Bathtub

I hear that some people clean the tub while taking a shower. Lathering up while spraying tile-cleaner doesn't cut it for me. When it's my turn to clean the tub, I take the spray bottle and wipe it down. It helps to get other family members on board by asking them to rinse the tub and give it a quick wipe-down after they use it.

To minimize tub clutter, buy bathroom caddies for each family member. Let them use their own personal carriers for washcloths, razors, soap, shampoo, and any other toiletries. No more bathtubs cluttered with everybody's personal soaps, and no more rings around all these items for you to clean.

Scour the Toilet

First, grab your choice of cleaner. Spray around, on top, and inside the bowl just to the water line. Clean it off with a paper towel. By the way, it might be a good idea to wear rubber gloves for this job. Next, pull out that handy-dandy toilet brush. If the bowl is really yucky, just pour in some straight bleach and let it sit about 10 minutes. Brush the inside until it looks pretty, or at least as pretty as the inside of a potty can look.

Make cleaning easier by not putting decorations on the flat area above the water tank. Items here not only collect dust, but also fall victim to backsplash.

A word of warning from my husband: please avoid using toilet tank drop-ins because they slowly eat away at the rubber gaskets in the plumbing. When you least expect it, the gaskets will fail and cause the toilet to overflow. That is one mess you won't want to clean up!

Mop the Floor

This is the area I despise the most because of the small space combined with odd-shaped fixtures that need cleaning behind. This requires a little extra elbow grease in the form of the good, old-fashioned hands and knees method. Maintain the floor during the week with some bathroom tissue. Wet it slightly and pick up what you can with it.

Give the Bathroom a Second Look

Is there anything you forgot? Give the bathroom a quick inspection and take care of any areas you missed. Make sure soap is available for washing hands. Hang a clean towel for drying hands. Straighten wall hangings that look crooked.

BEDROOM STRATEGY

What do you use your bedroom for? Sure, it is the place we sleep, but it has become the multi-purpose room for many homes. Not just for sleeping anymore, we use the bedroom as an exercise studio, a home office, a storage facility, and much more. Sometimes we even use it as a kitchen.

Let's think about assigning a function for the bedroom. How about using it just to sleep—or at least primarily for bed rest.

One thing that makes bedrooms in model homes so appealing is the design. We don't see bulky exercise equipment or unsightly filing cabinets. Stacks of bins and boxes don't fill closets or cover the floor.

Let's de-clutter the bedroom by transforming it from a multi-purpose room into a spa-like palace of rest and relaxation.

Pick up the Trash

What litter loiters in your bedroom? Remove any dirty dishes and take them immediately to the kitchen. Throw out empty soda bottles, clothes tags, old magazines, and any other trash.

If this is an area where important papers are mixed in with junk mail or paperwork, throw out the obvious trash. Box up papers you needing to sort to go through later.

Make the Bed

A neatly made bed is a great keep-it-clean motivator. There's something about having a focal point of eye-catching clean. Select a matching comforter set for a cleaner look. When linens match, the room looks less cluttered.

Check the bed linens. How many blankets and top sheets do you use to make the bed? Do you really need them all? Think about replacing those layers with one warm comforter. When I stopped using a top sheet and blanket, the bed got made more often. It decreased my laundry loads and added more space in the closet for other things. Double bonus there! Minimizing bedding not only means less stuff to clean and care for, but it decreases time spent making the bed.

Before making the bed, consider the last time the sheets tumbled around in soapy suds. If it's been more than a week, put them in the washer. Use hot water with bleach to kill bed bugs nestled in the fabric. While the linens get laundered, continue cleaning the bedroom.

Attack Piles of Clothing and Accessories

Overwhelmed by all the clothes, shoes, belts, hats, bows, sashes, and costume jewelry? I know how you feel. But then I discovered fewer clothes equated to less laundry. And fewer shoes mean less to trip over. Let go of outdated fashions. If it doesn't flatter or fit, donate it to charity. If something isn't comfortable to wear, don't keep it. Get rid of items with holes, stains, tears, missing buttons, or broken zippers.

Although makeup and perfume are not technically accessories, they tend to accessorize our dressers. Take a moment to de-clutter these and other personal grooming items. Test perfumes for their scent. Some dematerialize faster than others, leaving them with an alcohol-base aroma. Throw away lotions with odd colors or globs of hard material in them. A good rule of thumb for open makeup is to toss anything that's been open for a year or more; eye makeup has a shorter life span—three to six months—due to bacteria growth. Don't hesitate to throw away unopened makeup that's been sitting around for a while.

Clear Flat Surfaces

Just as cluttered counters make a kitchen look messy, cluttered dressers give the appearance of disorder. Keep a minimal amount of decorative items on your dressers. Try to keep the dresser tops as clear as possible. It gives the room a more spacious feel, plus makes the dressers easier to keep clean.

Organize the Closet and Dresser Drawers

Make homes for your clothing and accessories. Treat them with respect. Don't just throw them in a drawer or a closet.

Assign specific items to your dresser. I once stored all sorts of things in my dresser—makeup, lotions, books, stationery, important papers and junk mail, money, gift items, you name it. When I needed a place to put my clothes, junk had stolen the space. Remember the purpose of your dresser—clothes only.

A friend gave me this great piece of advice: use only one dresser. Limit items to clothes that don't need to be folded such as undergarments and socks. Using a standard dresser with four drawers, divide them in this way:

Drawer 1: Undergarments and socks

Drawer 2: Bed clothes

Drawer 3: Winter seasonal (heavy sweaters)

Drawer 4: Summer seasonal (shorts and swimwear)

Change this formula to meet your needs. If you have extra drawers, design it so that it's easy to keep things folded and looking neat. A T-shirt drawer tends to become disorderly and draws more effort to straighten, but folding jeans takes little time and energy.

Let's take a look at the closet. Try to keep the floor completely clear. It's too easy for junk—and valuables—to get pushed to the back in no-man's land. Unless you have a walk-in closet, it gets difficult to find matching shoes with bunches of other stuff on the closet floor.

It's much easier and takes less time to hang clothes rather than fold them. Look in your dresser and determine what needs to be moved to the closet. Here is a list of items to get you started: Pants, skirts, dresses, blouses, T-shirts, sleeveless tops, vests, and blazers.

Try organizing your closet by the color of the clothes. Put all black tops, pants, and skirts together. Work the continuum of darkest to lightest, ending with whites. Put rubber bands around shoe pairs to avoid lost mates.

A word on hangers. Avoid buying hangers of different colors. And forget about trying to color-coordinate clothes according to the hanger color. It takes more time matching things up—time that you don't want to spend every day organizing. Plus, a rainbow hanger effect gives the closet a more chaotic appearance. Keep it simple.

Sweep or Vacuum the Floor

Don't forget to clean under the bed. Evict dust bunnies and other debris squatting under the box spring.

I find that if I put one thing under the bed, other items magically appear there. As one dirty plate in the kitchen sink invites more dishes, junk under the bed accumulates the same way. Some of my neat-freak friends get away with storing gift wrap or shoes under the bed. For people like me, this area becomes a breeding ground for too much stuff. Make a rule to keep the floor under the bed clear of clutter.

If it's been a while since you've swept or vacuumed under the furniture, go ahead and do it. You never know what kind of clutter you might find.

Give the Bedroom a Second Look

Step back and take a look at everything. Did you miss anything? Do your last minute straightening and fluffing. Enjoy your new oasis of rest. Sweet dreams!

SOMETHING TO THINK ABOUT

- What does your kitchen, bedroom, and bathroom look like today? Do you keep suitably sized wastebaskets in these rooms so that garbage doesn't track on the floors? What is the main source of clutter in each room?
- How much kitchenware do you own? How much do you actually use in a typical week? What are you willing to part with?
- Do you overbuy when it comes to food? How can you change your shopping habits so you don't waste money and add clutter from purchasing food you don't need?
- What does your bedspread look like? Is it in better condition than just usable? Do you find the color and style attractive? Does it need to be replaced?
- What does your shower curtain look like? Do your towels and bathmats match the bathroom colors? Do they have a clean look or do they appear worn? What do you need to change to make your bathroom feel like a relaxing spa?

HOMEBUILDING

Therefore put on the full armor of God, so that when the day of evil comes, you may be able to stand your ground, and after you have done everything, to stand. Stand firm then, with the belt of truth buckled around your waist, with the breastplate of righteousness in place, and with your feet fitted with the readiness that comes from the gospel of peace. In addition to all this, take up the shield of faith, with which you can extinguish all the flaming arrows of the evil one. Take the helmet of salvation and the sword of the Spirit, which is the word of God. —Ephesians 6:13-17

There is a spiritual element in our battle against clutter. As you wage your war against too much stuff, remember to wear spiritual armor. Invite God into the process. Ask Him to help you defeat emotional attachments to material possessions. Seek His guidance as you develop your own strategy to create a dwelling place that is clean and comfortable.

5 PAPER WARFARE

EVER feel as if you're besieged by papers? I know how you feel. Bank statements, bills, magazine subscriptions, newsletters, newspapers, sales circulars, coupons, and credit offers target my home, and they all need to be sorted, de-cluttered, and organized. But the list doesn't stop there. There are store receipts, check stubs, school papers, work papers, clothing tags, grocery bags, packaging, notepad sheets, copy paper, and greeting cards.

Dealing with paper clutter is like battling waves of water flooding a ship filled with holes. We are the captains of our ships—our homes—and we need to remove the "water" so we don't sink in a sea of paper.

In a real ship, we'd plug the holes to keep additional water from coming in, bail the excess water, and set up a system to control water flow on the ship. The same strategy works with paper.

First, let's arm ourselves with some supplies:

Filing cabinets provide safe homes for important documents scattered around in different drawers, closets, and other hiding places. The best kind is one with all-locking drawers. I learned that lesson when my baby discovered how to open drawers and threw a paper-flinging party.

When filing papers, use manila folders and put them inside the green hanging file folders. Don't forget to label your folders.

A paper shredder is a must in this day and age for protection against identity theft. One little credit card offer in the wrong hands can cause big problems.

Young children often enjoy shredding papers, so you might want to consider delegating the task. As you review documents for tossing, let your child or grandchild work beside you and shred them.

A calendar and address book are wise investments. Which is better—the digital kind or the old-fashioned paper kind? The answer is the one that works best for you. If you go digital, make a backup in case your computer crashes. As you come across bills, write the due date in your calendar. Mark birthdays and appointments you want to remember, and throw out the reminder notes written on scrap paper. It's time to toss all those old envelopes you're keeping for the return address labels. Put that information in your address book.

STOP UNNECESSARY PAPER FROM ENTERING YOUR HOME

How does paper enter your home? These are the holes you need to plug. Get your name off mailing lists. Cancel unwanted magazine and newspaper subscriptions. Stop purchasing take-out dinners and fast food.

ELIMINATE EXCESS PAPER ALREADY IN YOUR HOME

Attacking the paper that floods your home is like draining the water already inside the ship. You need to bail the excess papers so you can get control of your home.

One of the biggest problems I faced when attempting to organize my papers was determining what to keep. I thought I'd play it safe and keep absolutely everything. But *everything* is really a lot of stuff. Imagine moving boxes upon boxes of papers every time you change residences. That's exactly what I did.

So what do we need to keep? Let's start with the things to keep permanently. These are called vital records, and they include:

- Birth and death certificates
- Adoption papers
- Marriage certificates
- Divorce and annulment decrees
- Vaccination records
- Wills

The toughest decisions for me were determining papers necessary to keep for tax purposes. Check with your tax advisor for a complete list, but here is the general guide. Keep the following tax related items for seven years:

- Year-end bank statements
- Dividend payment records
- Investment sales records
- Charitable contributions
- Credit statements
- Income tax returns
- W-2s
- Pension plan and retirement account records
- Loan agreements, payment books, and statements of discharge
- Cancelled checks and receipts for tax deductible items
- Medical receipts

If you have additional questions on what to save, visit the Internal Revenue Service Web site at irs.gov or call IRS help lines at 1-800-829-1040 for individual tax questions or 1-800-829-4933 for business tax questions. Ask for publication 552, titled *Record Keeping for Individuals*.

Papers that needlessly flounder in our homes many times relate to items we no longer own. Keep the following for as long as you own the items:

- Automobile records
- Insurance policies

- Investment purchase invoices
- Property bills of purchase

And last, there are those papers we keep for personal reasons:

- Magazines: Put away the notion of someday reading the stack of magazines going back eight years. Articles get recycled every year. There's always another cool craft project, exciting new diet, and awesome date night idea in the latest issues. Unless you have a work-related reason for holding on to back issues of magazines, keep only the last month's and current month's issues.
- Books: Don't we all love them? But must we keep fiction novels after we've already read them? Are you really going to read them again? Let me tell you about this amazing thing called a library. We don't have to clutter our homes with books when we can borrow them like we would a video. In fact, you can rent movies and CDs at most libraries too. Part with all your fiction (okay, most of it). Keep only the non-fiction works you know you will reference in the future. Review your cookbooks and evaluate if you honestly use them all. Also, consider purchasing an electronic reader such as a Nook or Kindle for easy access to lots of books that won't take up lots of space.
- Old school papers: Our parents saved all our school work from kindergarten on up. Then we save everything from our college years. Limit school papers to those that have relevance in your life today. If you insist on keeping some as memorabilia, pick out the ones you like most and put them in a scrapbook. But don't keep everything. In fact, if you have no emotional connection to your alma maters, why not let go of the yearbooks while you're at it?
- Bad photographs: Why is it we can't get ourselves to toss pictures with a loved one's head chopped off, red-eye problems in every retina, and major focus issues? It's time for these bad quality photos to meet the trash. Don't be shy about getting rid of unflattering photos and excess duplicates either. Press delete on

your digital camera when you capture a fuzzy image. Consider investing in digital archiving of old photos.

- Personal correspondence: Be selective on the letters and greeting cards you keep. Is the card from someone who is now or at one time was an important person in your life? Did the sender write a personal message in the card or just scribble a signature? Do the letters fill you with delight or make your soul weep? Would the next generation find them a burden or enjoy them as a part of their heritage? Use this same criteria when evaluating digital communication of a personal nature.

Let's start attacking those papers. Begin by tossing the trash. Thin out your paper boxes by eliminating the no brainers like old catalogs, sales circulars, newspapers, coupons, and junk mail. Be mindful of throwing away anything containing personal information, especially documents containing anyone's social security number. Use a shredder to maintain privacy and protect yourself from fraud. When sorting mounds of paper, create a shred box to shred all at once.

After sifting out the trash from potentially important papers, put papers on the same topic together. Depending on the amount of papers, separate by topic in boxes, folders, or with paper clips. Keep anything questionable, but toss what you know is not necessary to keep. You will determine the destiny of any questionable items in your next sort, before filing the stacks of papers.

For big de-cluttering jobs involving mail, open envelopes and place the correspondence in stacks by category for you to examine. Find a helper to open the envelopes while you review what's inside them. Tossing the envelopes alone will cut your paper job in half.

Whatever you do, do not blindly throw boxes of papers away. Check for hidden cash, uncashed payroll checks, savings bonds, and other forgotten treasures. Who knows? Irreplaceable photographs may have found their way into one of those boxes of papers. Know what you are throwing out before you get rid of things. And again, shred papers with personal information—or at least tear them into small pieces.

SET UP A SYSTEM

Prepare your paper filing tools for use. You will need:
- Four-drawer locking filing cabinet
- Manila folders
- Green hanging file folders
- Pens for labeling

I will give the information to create a basic filing system. Once you're reasonably organized, you can experiment with color-coded folders, fancy labels, and other more elaborate organizing techniques.

When creating a filing system, define categories for filing your papers. Label the main categories and develop subheadings under them. I found it confusing and overwhelming when I read all the potential categories and subheadings as I studied paper management. To simplify this process, I will show you what I did to create a system that works for me.

1. Identify the main areas of paper clutter. We all have Vital Documents and Financials, so plan on including these two categories as a given.

2. Create a section titled Monthly Bills. Although this technically fits under Financials, this receives its own category because of its fluid and active nature. File bills, marking the check number and payment date right on the invoice. Record the confirmation number if given one and file it.

3. Evaluate the activities that fill your calendar and analyze the paper flow associated with each activity. Being highly involved in church, I felt this was a large enough area to demand its own category. As a writer, I have tons of work-related documents mingling in the house, so I created a separate category titled Writing.

4. Insert a Personal category for hobbies and special interests. I like coming up with fun and innovative party and gift ideas, so I keep

a folder for this topic. Christmas is my favorite holiday, and I enjoy making holiday plans and exploring new traditions. Christmas easily merits its own folder.

5. Allocate enough room for family members to file their own papers. Better yet, purchase a filing cabinet for each family member. Teach each person to be responsible for his or her own paperwork. Consider getting a two drawer filing cabinet for children to use so you don't have to worry about them touching any of your important papers.

Use my example as a blueprint, modifying the categories to meet your lifestyle.

Financial

Place a large label on the file folder to identify where the financial section begins, doing the same for each subsequent category. I keep separate folders for the following:

- Individual tax years (Contains copy of tax forms, W2s, end of year statements, and receipts for deductions)
- Tax Prep (Contains W2s and yearly statements as they are received, as well as receipts for itemized deductions)
- Investments and Retirement Accounts
- Credit Reports (Includes any correspondence to fix errors)
- Real Estate (Home purchase and repairs)
- Insurance Documents

Vital Records

Keep original records in a safe deposit box or fire-proof safe. File copies at home for easy access. Add folders for items that apply to you such as adoption or divorce certificates and other legal records.

- Birth, Marriage, and Death Certificates
- Immunization Records
- Medical Records
- Veterinary Records
- Resumes
- Wills
- Genealogy (Copies of vital documents from deceased relatives)

Tax Receipts

Keeping a separate file for current year tax receipts makes figuring deductions easier. I don't worry about making a separate file for medical receipts and a separate file for charity receipts. I just want them all together. Paper clip receipts together by type if that extra step helps you stay organized. For me, it's easier to sort them at tax time. If you own your own business, go ahead and label separate folders for personal deductions and business deductions.

Make it easier to track cash register receipts by making a copy of the receipt. Then toss the receipt and write the details on the copy regarding what you bought and what you used it for. Some cash register ink lightens and disappears with time. This protects you from saving documents that become useless because you can't read the numbers on them.

Monthly Bills

I wrestled with filing bills under their own headings such as phone, utilities, cable, etc., or filing them according to the month. Ultimately, I decided to file each bill under its own heading, but I try to keep the most current bill in front. Save no more than one year's worth of statements, unless you need them for tax purposes. How do you know if you need them for income tax reasons? Only if you are using them for itemized deductions like a cell phone plan purchased for a business.

Church

This is for church activities or any activity that generates paper flow. Here are my spiritual paper makers:
• Ministry
• Bible Study

Writing

Writing is akin to a work-related heading. Do you own a home business? Do you bring your work home? Instead of a writing cat-

egory, create a title that reflects your work. Here is how I break down my writing category:
- Story Ideas
- Contracts
- Marketing and Publicity
- Conferences
- Writers Groups

Personal

What are your hobbies? Consider having a file for travel, recipes, fitness, decorating, or other areas of interest. These are a few of mine:
- Party and Gift Ideas
- Christmas
- Community Calendar

Family

I created this category so other family members could do their own filing. My husband files his own work papers and hobby related papers. My son has a two-drawer filing cabinet of his own for school-work and enrichment activities, however I manage the filing cabinet for him. If given free reign, he'd designate it as a toy chest.

On a side note, as a home educator, I found it helpful to dedicate a two-drawer filing cabinet toward lesson planning. At this time, I need only one drawer for papers. I use the second drawer to store supplies.

If your children attend public school, consider giving them a two-drawer filing cabinet as a tool to teach paper management. Give them a file folder for each subject they study. Add folders for field trips, sports, and enrichment activities. If your children are active in church, give them a folder for handouts from Sunday School, youth group, Children's Choir, or whatever the activity. If the ministry activity generates a lot of paper, give it its own folder. Otherwise, just label it "Church." Your child's cabinet might look something like this:
- Math
- Language Arts

- Social Studies
- Science
- Spelling
- Spanish
- Specials (Art, Music, PE)
- Field Trips (include permission slips and information about the field trip itself)
- Baseball (file team rosters, schedules, and other take home papers)
- Piano Lessons (worksheets, song sheets)
- Scouts (fundraisers, calendars, contact lists)
- Church (Sunday School handouts, event flyers, newsletters)

Once you identify your main categories and label your folders with subheadings, sort through your papers again as you file them. Set a goal of organizing at least one box of papers per day. Expect to take a couple weeks to several months building a working filing system. It all depends on how many papers you have and how fast new ones come in.

BEYOND THE FILING CABINET

Not every paper we own needs to be filed, but we still may need to keep them for a short time. We need a *paper flow* system to prevent a tsunami of paper from overtaking our homes. Let's view paper flow in terms of the new papers coming into our home. What do we do with them before we file or toss them?

When you collect your mail each day, toss the junk mail right away. Open your bills, eliminating the envelopes and unnecessary papers inside of them. Cash checks immediately. Don't save checks to keep from spending the money. If you want to save the money, cash the check and set the money aside in a safe place.

Bills

Beyond overall organization of paperwork, people who battle clutter also wrestle with bill paying. It's not necessarily because we don't have the money. We just have trouble keeping track of when we made the last payment and which payments are due now. Sometimes we misplace our statements, checkbooks, or remittance envelopes. We might even forget to balance our checkbooks, telling ourselves we'll send in the amount due after we determine if we have enough in our checking accounts to cover the payment. In the meantime, interest charges kick in and late fees accumulate.

What can we do to keep track of our bills without creating a detailed and cumbersome spreadsheet? For some people, bill tracking software on the computer works fine. An easier solution is a monthly at-a-glance reminder placed in a visible location. On a blank sheet of paper, list your monthly bills, amount due, and due date. After you pay the bill, record the amount paid and the date payment was sent. Include the check number and confirmation number, if applicable. This convenient tool gives you a quick big picture view of what's due and what's paid.

If I file a bill before it's paid, chances are it doesn't get paid. It needs to be in the open where I can see it and access it with ease. I designate a special place for bills in my kitchen. Use what works for you. Designate a letter tray just for bills. Hang a wooden letter holder on the wall. Try a calendar with pockets. Put your statements in a basket on your kitchen counter. If the method you use stops working, try something else.

Once paid, the only reason I save old bills is to track costs. If rates increase, I check the previous month to compare charges. It makes it easy for me to negotiate new rates when I know what they offered in the past. With most bills now accessible online, I'm more likely to toss non-business-related paper statements after I make the monthly payment.

School Work

When I give workshops, parents often ask what to do with their kids' *current* schoolwork. Sometimes teachers forget to record a grade, so it's not a bad idea to save papers—just not forever. After the school year ends, save only creative works, not math facts or multiple choice worksheets. Pick the best to save.

For example, at seven-years-old, my son created his own rendition of Van Gogh's "Starry Night." It's a beautiful piece of art. Instead of sticking it in a folder and storing it in the back of a closet, I had it matted and framed to hang in a prominent place in my home. I want him to know that his works of art mean more to me than something I can buy at the store.

Invitations

In my household, recording a social engagement on the calendar is not enough. My husband doesn't always check it. Nor is there enough room to copy directions or phone numbers. I still mark the event on the calendar, but I either attach the invitation to the fridge with a magnet or place it in a designated basket. When marking these on my computer calendar, I schedule event reminders too.

Coupons

I occasionally use coupons. For most restaurants, I store coupons in a plastic pencil bag. It stands out more than a regular envelope. Plus, it won't rip. On those occasions when we opt to eat dinner out, we decide on where we want to go—or the type of cuisine we're in the mood for—and then check for a coupon. Unless we're short on cash, I don't want a coupon dictating where we go for dinner. Rather than letting coupons clutter my purse, I keep the restaurant coupon bag in a drawer in the kitchen.

If coupons are for a place we visit often, I keep them in my wallet but limit their number to prevent overload. My family loves Chick-Fil-A. We go there a lot, so it makes sense to keep my Chick-Fil-A coupons accessible for those scheduled and spur-of-the-moment trips.

Giving restaurant and grocery coupons separate homes prevents them from getting mixed up with each other, and that makes life easier. I shop at a certain health food store that publishes a bi-monthly coupon magazine. Since I shop at this store about every week, I keep these coupons in an envelope in my purse and toss them when they expire. I save only the coupons for the items I buy regularly. I don't save the other ones "just in case."

Set up a coupon system. Don't cut every coupon available. Some people use specialized coupon wallets or index card holders. Others do an Internet search before shopping and print out the coupon. Still others find that coupons cause clutter no matter what they do and choose not to use them at all.

Make Technology Work for You

Look for ways to make technology work for you in order to decrease the amount of paper in your home. Consider dedicating an e-mail account for digital sales flyers from stores and small businesses. If you belong to business associations, request they e-mail you newsletters instead of sending them in the mail. Rather than cutting out coupons from the Sunday paper, print out the coupon from the digital ad if and when you need it.

As the use of e-mail increases, you may not need so many paper file folders. You don't need to make a copy of all your e-mail correspondence and attachments. Save digital or soft copies of important e-mails and delete the rest. Print out e-mails only if necessary.

Use the same principle for organizing paper files to create a filing system on your computer. Let's use e-mail as our example. When you receive snail mail, what do you do? You toss the junk mail. When you open your inbox, delete the spam. Just as you would with your paper documents, set aside time to purge your digital documents.

File your e-mail as you would any other paperwork. Create folders according to their topic such as small group, school, work, and family correspondence. When you enroll your children in activities, create e-mail folders for each activity. If more than one child participates in the same activity at different levels, then create sub-folders. If you enroll your two boys in Scouts and one is a bear cub while the other is a wolf cub, you will be more organized by giving them separate folders. For grandparents, consider creating folders for each of your children so that when they e-mail you pictures of the grandkids and other personal correspondence you can keep track of everyone.

No matter how much we turn to our computers to create a paperless society, there are still papers to file. We must know how to do both to live a well-organized life.

SOMETHING TO THINK ABOUT

- How many years' worth of papers are you storing? What would be okay to get rid of?
- What questions do you have about keeping certain papers for tax purposes? Write them down and contact a certified public accountant for advice.
- Do you have a filing system in place? If you do, how can you change it to make it more efficient? If you don't, how do you plan to start one?
- Do you have a paper flow system in place for papers not ready to be filed? What strategies help you track current bills, bank statements, invitations, and other time-sensitive papers?
- How are you incorporating technology into your battle to control paper flow?

 ## HOMEBUILDING

Let love and faithfulness never leave you; bind them around your neck, write them on the tablet of your heart. —Proverbs 3:3

What do you write on the tablet of your heart? Does it contain a to-do list of good deeds to perform? Are there scoreboards for repaying kindness and hurt? Or does it hold reminders of God's love and faithfulness?

Let's de-clutter the filing cabinets in our hearts. Instead of creating lists of things to do, let God start doing things with you. Toss away the relationship checklists and stop keeping score. Think about finding a verse in Scripture that speaks to your heart. Write it on the tablet of your heart by memorizing it so you can access it any time.

6 ESCAPE FROM LAUNDRY MOUNTAIN

IS keeping up with the laundry a major battle in your home? If you feel overwhelmed by the amount of clothes needing to be washed, select a day to do nothing but laundry.

First, gather your laundry. It's funny how clothing finds its way into almost any room. Take an empty laundry basket to areas hit by clothing missiles. Think of your hamper as a waste basket for clothing.

In cases of severe laundry bombardment, you might consider packing everything in your car and taking it to a Laundromat. If you are so far behind on laundry that it will take a week of non-stop clothes washing to catch up, this will get you caught up fast. It will cost more, but you can complete ten or more loads in less than a few short hours.

As you focus on clothing and linens, take time to de-clutter so there will be less laundry in the future.

FROM PLAYPENS TO MOUNTAIN RANGES

"I don't have anything to wear!"

"I hardly have any clothes!"

"I can never find an outfit I like!"

Sound familiar? Do you complain about your lack of clothing, yet your overstuffed closets and dressers tell a different story?

When I was growing up, my mother always had a mountain of laundry to wash. She kept a playpen in the basement where all the dirty clothes piled up. I don't think she ever saw the bottom of the playpen after she started using it as a laundry basket. Add to that several large pails of dirty linens. I'm not talking about a kitchen-sized pail that one keeps under the sink. I'm talking about the enormous trash totes that one leaves in front of the house on garbage day.

Do you struggle with mountainous piles of laundry? I once had that struggle too. But I didn't use a playpen. My dirty clothes just got thrown on the floor.

Then one day it occurred to me that the fewer clothes I owned, the fewer clothes I would need to wash.

Fillers (socks and undergarments)

Let's start with what I call *fillers*. These are the smaller items that lurk in the piles of clothes. These are also some of the easiest to part with since most of us don't develop emotional attachments to things like socks and underwear. When it came to fillers, socks were my downfall.

How many lonesome socks do you have lying around? If there was a mating service for the collection of single socks that lingered in my home, someone could have become rich.

Rather than dealing with the hassle of pairing up my socks, I would buy new ones. Of course, I never threw the old ones away. It's not like when we gain weight, we gain a sock size. I had no reason to throw them out.

One day I decided to just toss them all with the exception of a handful of pairs. My plan was to start fresh. I bought two new packs of the same style and color. Less work to mate them after they're washed, right?

A king-size trash bag full of nothing but socks testified to the mental weight and physical mass of fillers. Socks of all different styles and colors overwhelmed me when I thought about all the laundry waiting for me to wash and partner.

Keeping it simple helped me prevent the extra work of sock care.

What can you do about your sock fillers? Consider tossing some if you have too many. Just find a place for them in the trash. Hold on to only what you need. And please, don't try to find other uses for them. Sure, you can use an old sock for cleaning, but the goal is decluttering. Once you have a handle on your stuff, then you can start thinking about repurposing items for other uses. Remember, we can't keep it all and keep a clean house!

Now let's talk about underwear. Here is the deal with undergarments. Put in the trash the ones with holes, poor elasticity, tears, and stains. Don't worry about washing them first. If you wash them, you might be tempted to wear them. We don't want them to get mixed up with the good stuff.

Plus, we are too valuable to be wearing things that belong in the trash. Let's treat ourselves with dignity and respect. If an item of clothing is so worn that it projects a low self-worth, just throw it out.

Ill-fitting Clothes

"This makes me look fat!"

"Nothing fits!"

"I can't wear that—it emphasizes all the wrong places!"

Have you ever said or thought that about your clothes? Come on, there must be something you own that is flattering. That beautiful outfit is probably hiding somewhere in all those piles of laundry!

So if you own all these clothes that don't work, why do you insist on keeping them? I know! They might fit someday. Or you can use the ones that fit for painting, right?

It's time to assess priorities. How important is it to defeat the laundry monster and bring this mountain of dirty clothes down to a manageable size?

Start with the piles of clean clothes. Ask yourself, *Do I really love it?* as you evaluate each item. Set aside anything that doesn't fit or flatter. Be sure to put those items in a box or bag that will not become mixed with the ones you want to keep. Immediately take donation items to the drop off centers before you think of an excuse to keep them.

Laundry Piles

Still have too many clothes? It's time to start putting "friends" together. Let's start with T-shirts. It's easy to accumulate lots of these. Find all your T-shirts. Pull them out of your dressers, closets, clothes baskets, and other hiding places. Folding them neatly, find a large surface to rest them on. Assess exactly what you have. Did you think only about fifteen or so were out of sight only to discover the number is closer to fifty?

It's hard to accurately assess what to get rid of when we don't realize exactly how much we have. Do this with other clothing items as well.

Wardrobes

What is your "style"? Think about the image you wish to portray by the clothes you wear. If an item doesn't fit with your style, consider tossing it. In the movie, My Big Fat Greek Wedding, Tula tells her love interest that when they first met she was "frump girl." Whatever style you choose, like Tula, let's put away frump girl.

What says *beautiful* to you? There are many styles of beautiful. What looks nice on you may look like a fashion blunder on me. Keep the clothes that make you feel good when you wear them. What ones do you feel most confident in? What ones make you look most attractive?

Let me share a story on this. I love sweat pants because they are so comfortable; but they do not say beautiful. While channel surfing one day, I came across a talk show episode where the theme was "I married a hot mama, but now all she wears is sweats!" I wondered if I could have been one of the women on that show. That was enough motivation for change. I didn't need so many sweat pants, so I decided to keep a couple pairs specifically for the gym and got rid of the rest.

What types of clothes do you need? Think about your lifestyle. How often do you dress up? Does work require fine business wear, casual wear, or something in between? What outfits are best suited for your hobbies and interests? Be realistic by matching clothing styles to your lifestyle.

What items are easiest to clean? Dry-clean only means more work. We may not actually be laundering these clothes ourselves, but we still have to drop them off and pick them up, not to mention the cost of having them cleaned. Keep items that require dry-cleaning to a minimum.

What items are most versatile? These are the classics and tend to be solid colors that can be worn with a variety of items. They are not faddish or trendy, but stay in style. They can dress down a business outfit or dress up a pair of jeans.

Linens

If all we had to wash were clothes, we'd have a lot less to clean. But we still have towels, tablecloths, curtains, bedding, and other linens. If they are not bogging us down in the laundry room, they are stealing valuable storage space. Prepare to cast out the villainous linens that create loads of work.

How many towels do you need for each person living in your household anyway? I suggest starting with a maximum of seven, one for each day of the week. If you can do with less, then go for it. When I started de-cluttering, I kept about four for each member of my family. That seemed to work out pretty well. Keeping fewer towels may mean you have to wash them more often, but at least you won't have a mountain of them always waiting to be washed.

Do you use tablecloths? How many do you really need to keep? I discovered it was much easier to clean my table with a sponge after each meal rather than to constantly wash tablecloths. Figure out what works best for you.

How many sets of bed sheets is enough? My vote is two for each bed. This way when you wash your bedding, you can make your bed with a clean set right away. It's a good idea to keep a few extra blankets for cold winter nights, overnight guests, or snuggling while watching your favorite television show.

Clothing and Linen Guidelines

When determining which clothing and other linens to keep, ask the following questions:

- Is it ripped or torn?
- Is it frayed or faded?
- Are there missing buttons or broken zippers?
- Is it permanently stained?
- Does it fit?
- Does it flatter?
- Does it match with anything?
- Does it wrinkle easily?
- Does it need to be dry-cleaned?
- Do I have enough similar items that perform the same job?
- Do I really need it?
- Do I really love it?

Washing Instructions

Part of de-cluttering and organizing the laundry includes actually doing the wash. For years, I washed all my clothes in cold water because I didn't know what was safe to wash in higher temperatures. I never learned how to use bleach in the laundry, so I settled for dingy whites. But after de-cluttering my clothes to a point where only the good ones were left, I wanted to know the right way to do laundry so I could take care of my things. After interviewing friends with laundry expertise, I learned that there is no one right way to do laundry. There are, however, some general guidelines.

Let's start with supplies. Every laundry room needs the following:

- Laundry detergent: liquid or powder, it doesn't matter.
- Bleach: use one-half cup bleach when washing whites.
- Bleach pen: this works great on whites that can't be bleached because of colored emblems or stripes.
- Trigger spray stain remover: use a color-safe spray-on bleach to remove stains on colors not safe for regular bleach.

You might also consider these optional supplies.

- Color booster: these are the "oxy" products that add an extra cleaning element to colors.
- Fabric softener or fabric sheets: I ran out of these one day and stopped using them. Not using them seemed to make no difference. For my dad, these are a must. You may want them too.

Before washing, always do the following:

- Check pockets for things such as money and lipstick. I shudder to think of the loads I ruined because of a lipstick left in a pocket.
- Close zippers, snaps, and hooks. This protects other garments in the same wash load.
- Tie drawstrings. Trust me, pushing a string back out a centimeter at a time because the string got lost in the seams is no fun.
- Remove unwashable belts, pins, and other accessories attached to garments.
- Pre-treat stains. Follow instructions on the stain-treating product you use.
- Mend clothes with tears, broken zippers, missing buttons. Agitation from the washer can turn a small mending job into a major one.
- Check care labels on garments for special washing or drying instructions.

What Is Permanent Press Anyway?

Most washers and dryers have a permanent press setting. When interviewing moms about their laundry routines, I was surprised to hear so many answers along the lines of "I don't know what that's for." Use the permanent press setting for clothing that tends to wrinkle. In the washer, this setting offers a cool down period before the final rinse to prevent wrinkles. In the dryer, the difference is the heat setting—it's not quite as hot as the heavy setting. Again, this prevents wrinkles from forming in the dryer.

Use higher heat settings for denims, towels, and garments that don't easily wrinkle. Set the dryer to fluff air for delicates—or better yet, air-dry them.

Prep Work

Everyone sorts laundry a little differently, but it all breaks down to whites, lights, and darks. For easier sorting, keep three baskets in your laundry room for each color sort.

The rule of thumb for washing is the lighter the color, the hotter the water. Check all care labels on garments for special washing or drying instructions. Hot water may be too harsh for a delicate white. Delicate knits sometimes need to be air-dried.

Start the first load doing whites that require bleach. Then move to whites and off-whites without bleach. Continue with colors from lightest to darkest. This helps prevent bleach particles that may have escaped the final rinse from ruining colors. Do not pour detergent directly on clothing when loading the washer. Remember—never overload your washer.

Whites

Whites include undergarments, sock, towels, and linens. Use a hot water wash. First, add bleach. Let it mix a little with the water, and then add soap. After the water finishes filling the washer and the agitator starts, add the clothes.

Lights

For whites and off-whites such as blouses, skirts, and pants, use a warm water wash. Don't add bleach.

Darks

Use cold water wash for colors. Do not add bleach. Turn clothing inside out to prevent bleeding and fading. Wash new clothes separately if they are in colors or fabrics that tend to run. Or wash them with like colors if bleeding on to like colors is not a concern. If I purchase a new red top, I like to hand wash it by itself first. Then I feel comfortable adding it with a load of reds or darks.

If you live in a small home, you may not have the room for separate laundry hampers to sort colors. I found the easiest way to work in small spaces is to use two baskets—one for undergarments and socks and one for everything else.

THE DRYER

Check the lint trap before you start your load in case the last person to use the dryer forgot to clean it. Fill the dryer, but don't overstuff it. Toss in a fabric softener sheet if you like to use them and turn the dryer on.

Fold and hang clothes immediately when dry. Don't give yourself more work by allowing clothing to wrinkle in the dryer once the dryer stops.

The thing I love most about doing laundry is that most of it involves *passive* cleaning. I put the clothes in the wash machine and then do whatever I want for the next thirty to forty minutes. Taking clothes out of the dryer, folding them and putting them away only takes a few minutes. Set your timer to see how fast you can sort, fold, and put away clothes. I bet it's quicker than you think. Before you know it, that mountain of laundry will be down to almost nothing.

SOMETHING TO THINK ABOUT

- Why do you have so much laundry? What kinds of clothes do you have too many of?
- What obstacles prevent you from de-cluttering your closets? What are you going to do about them?
- How will you evaluate the number of articles of clothing you should keep? Make a list of the number you think you need and compare it to how many you actually own.
- What kind of boundaries will you establish to prevent new clothing purchases from overloading your house?
- What can you do to simplify your laundry routine? How can other family members help out more by caring for their own laundry?

HOMEBUILDING

And why do you worry about clothes? See how the lilies of the field grow. They do not labor or spin. Yet I tell you that not even Solomon in all his splendor was dressed like one of these. If that is how God clothes the grass of the field, which is here today and tomorrow is thrown into the fire, will he not much more clothe you, O you of little faith? —Matthew 6:28-30

I consistently found excuses for keeping clothes that should have been tossed. *They might fit someday. They may come back in fashion. They cost good money.* What are some of your excuses? Yet God tells us not to worry about our wardrobes. He will clothe us in more splendor than we can imagine if we follow Him. It's time we stop worrying so much about our clothes and start trusting in God.

7 COMBATTING THE CLUTTER

LIVING rooms, dining rooms, dens, home offices, rec rooms, attics, basements, garages—even our vehicles—also cry for our attention. So do our drawers, cabinets, and totes, not to mention our yards.

ROOM BY ROOM

Start with the rooms that are used most often. Save your basement, attic, and other storage areas for last. Here is the general plan:

Toss the Trash

Do a quick clean sweep with a trash bag and throw out obvious garbage. Set aside items to donate to charity. Get donation items out of the house as quickly as possible.

Clear Flat Surfaces

Start with the visible clutter on tabletops, shelves, and floors. Last, move to the invisible clutter nesting inside drawers and storage bins. Send lost items home. Put homeless friends together, keeping similar things in boxes marked *sort*.

Clean Furniture and Accessories

Wash removable couch fabric and couch covers. Clean bureaus, coffee tables, and desks. Dust lamps, figurines, and other décor.

Sweep or Vacuum the Floor

If it's been a while, move furniture for a thorough cleaning. Get underneath and behind furniture. Consider hiring a professional carpet cleaner to give your carpets new life.

Check Your Work

Take a look at the room and tend to anything you missed.

Here is a review of what to do for extreme decluttering:

The first pass—toss trash. Throw out obvious trash. Set aside belongings for donation and drop them off at your local charity ASAP.

The second pass—group friends. Place things in boxes according to category. Put friends together—Christmas décor in one pile, clothes in another, papers in another, and so forth.

The third pass and on—sort and organize. Sort through individual items in each box and find homes for them or toss them.

After you've de-cluttered the mess, consider what you can do to make visually displeasing rooms less of an eyesore and easier to clean. In my childhood home, the laundry machines were kept in an unfinished basement. It felt dark and murky down there. Cobwebs hung from the wood and pipes. I didn't enjoy going down there. A neat, clean, finished look in areas such as the basement or attic adds to the overall appeal of a home and makes the chores you do there more enjoyable.

DE-CLUTTERING THE SMALL SPACES

Once visible clutter has been tackled and dealt with, it's time to focus on the collections hiding in drawers, cabinets, and totes.

How do the insides of your drawers and cabinets look? How many are organized? Which ones overflow with clutter? Analyze what does and doesn't work in each of them and learn from it. There's a reason most people use silverware trays. They effectively organize eating utensils.

And what about junk drawers—why create a place that becomes a home for clutter? These temporary shelters easily become permanent residences. One junk drawer can multiply into several. I tried setting up "his" and "hers" junk drawers for my husband and me, but when they became filled, there was nowhere else to stow the clutter. Rather than putting objects back in their assigned homes or making a decision on keeping them, we tossed everything in new junk drawers. They popped up everywhere, even in places that were previously organized. The junk spread to every available drawer and cabinet in my home.

What flounders in the bottom of your totes? Whether it's a gym bag, book bag, fanny pack, or purse, they all attract clutter. Common stowaways include runaway lipstick, forgotten packs of gum, scattered change, old receipts, lost checks, expired coupons, and the kitchen sink. Trash such as hair from brushes, food crumbs, and candy wrappers reside at the bottom like sticky refuse in a garbage can.

Drawers, cabinets, and totes are black holes where stuff disappears, never to see daylight again. To thoroughly clean them, we need to completely empty them. Use the following technique for de-cluttering all types of compartments:

Empty the Contents

Dump the entire contents from the compartment onto a clean surface, clear of clutter. Double-check corners and crevices. When de-cluttering purses, be sure to double-check all zipper compartments. For cabinets with multiple shelves, clear every shelf if possible. For larger cabinets, you may need to do one shelf at a time.

Toss the Trash

Get rid of the garbage. Take note of the types of trash your tote, drawer, or cabinet collects. Let's examine refuse that tends to lurk in purses and how to prevent it from accumulating:

- Sales flyers: When salespeople hand out brochures, do you accept them? Or does the marketing piece end up lining your purse? Learn to decline politely or immediately toss the handout in the nearest trash receptacle.
- Candy: What snacks do you carry in your purse? Think about limiting the types of quick pick-me-ups you store in your handbag to breath mints and gum. No candy means no melted chocolate, sugar pellets, or wrappers cluttering your purse. Your waistline will thank you.

- Receipts: Is your purse a dumping ground for every sales receipt and invoice you receive? Keep important receipts, invoices, and other related documents in a designated envelope. Toss the ones you don't need. File the items in this envelope on a weekly basis.

Send Lost Items Home

What do you have in your drawers, cabinets, and totes that belong somewhere else? Put those items away.

Remember the organizing rule of storing friends together. Assign like items to a specific place. Use organizing tools such as mesh trays and labels to help drawers and cabinets remain orderly.

For purses and totes, store makeup in one compartment. Keep your wallet, cash, and checks in another. If you don't have enough compartments for what you like to carry, use mini-bags for storing like items.

Clean the Empty Drawer, Cabinet, or Tote

Wash your purse or tote according to the material. Use a damp paper towel or sponge to clean drawers and shelves. Add soap or other cleaning agent for stubborn dirt.

Designate Drawers, Cabinets, and Totes for Specific Uses

As you decide what to store in these places that once housed clutter, consider the items that naturally gravitated into them. Do certain spaces tend to accumulate mostly office type clutter? If so, that might be a good place for office supplies. If the prescriptions in your medicine cabinet keep ending up in your kitchen cabinet, then clear a kitchen shelf for vitamins, medications, and other related items. Think about what you find in the clutter hotspots and work with the natural tendencies of where you place things.

GARAGE

Originally made for cars, garages today house everything under the sun. Lacking room for automobiles, our expensive cars sit in the driveway and our garages store assorted odds and ends of far lesser value.

It's time to clear out the garage and give it back to the cars.

- Get rid of the obvious trash.
- Group like items together to give you a big picture of how many of the same materials you own. As you sort through storage, ask yourself, *Do I really need this?*
- Set up an organizing system that gives homes to groups of items according to zones. Store friends together: gardening equipment against one wall, tools in another corner, automotive supplies on their own special shelf, and so forth.

Here are some ideas to make your garage more user-friendly:

- Make a Peg-Board for tools. Draw an outline in black marker to help you remember where each tool belongs.
- Create a workbench with cupboards and cabinets for construction supplies, but keep only those you need.
- Nail hooks in the wall to hang shovels and rakes.
- Seal cement garage floors. Sealant prevents clutter of the dust variety.
- Add drywall and/or a coat of paint for a finished look.

No matter how disorganized your garage looks, set a goal that it will always be clean enough to perform the function it was designed for—to protect your vehicles from outside elements. As you have the time, organize your garage and add those special touches to make it comfortable for you and your car.

Creating a beautiful home takes more than de-cluttering the inside of our houses and garages. Let's not forget about the extensions of our homes—our cars and our lawns.

AUTOMOBILES

Some people live in their cars—or at least a peek inside gives that impression. My car has always been a clutter magnet. With a trunk full of storage and a mess on the floorboards, I struggled with keeping this small area clean, let alone my entire house.

In a way, our cars are extensions of our homes. We use them as kitchens, chowing down our fast food dinners. Turning them into mobile powder rooms, we brush our hair and put on makeup, sometimes while driving in traffic. Newer models have DVD players attached, and they become living rooms on wheels. We also transform them into mobile home offices with Bluetooth accessories for working on-the-go. Sometimes, our cars even become mini bedrooms on long trips when we stop at a rest area for a quick nap.

Are you ready to transform your vehicle into a clean machine? Put a car care kit together to make it easier to clean and maintain these mini homes-on-wheels. Store your kit in an accessible area in the garage or in the trunk of your car. Please note that cars require special cleaning products because of the paint, waxes, finishes, and window tints. Here is what you need:

- Upholstery cleaner: Seats and floors get dirty. Use a special car-cleaning agent to remove tough grime such as Stoner Upholstery and Carpet Cleaner. These cleaners also work well on the inside of your home too.

- Interior cleaner: The dashboard, steering wheel, console, and other interior surfaces require cleaning. Whatever brand you use, verify that it's safe for all areas. I like Meguiar's Quik Interior Detailer because it works on all surfaces in my car.

- Extra-strength dirt remover: Keep a special cleaner on hand for hard-to-remove dirt such as tree sap, tar, and sticky bugs. I prefer Meguiar's Gold Class Bug & Tar Remover because it's a trigger spray. Other comparable cleaners tend to be in aerosol form and contain scary warnings about extreme flammability.

- Glass cleaner: Not every glass cleaner is safe for car windows. Find one you like in your favorite store's automotive department. My friends rave about Stoner Invisible Glass. It gets an A+ in my book too.
- Car wash soap: Regular dish soap can be harmful to automobile paint and finishes.
- Automotive washing mitt: It's kind of like an oven mitt, except it's used for cleaning cars.
- Cotton terry cloth or micro fiber towel: Use these for drying your car. Don't use rags or old, shoddy towels.

Start with the Trash

Throw out garbage on the seats and floors. Check for debris underneath the seats too. Don't forget the middle console, door pockets, glove compartment, and trunk.

Send Lost Items Home

Remove everything that doesn't belong in the car and send it to its proper place. Start with the visible clutter on the floor and seats. Then move to the area under the seats, in between crevices, and inside compartments.

Designate storage areas in your automobile for specific items. Begin with the glove compartment. Start by completely emptying it. Limit items that go back in the glove compartment to essential paperwork and maybe a couple of pens. Keep registration and insurance together. Use a bright colored envelope so you can find them easily if the glove compartment gets cluttered. Having the registration and insurance lost in a sea of papers is not good if you get pulled over. File car maintenance records in an envelope in the glove compartment so they are readily available if needed.

Side pockets on doors serve as clutter bunkers. Just because you have a door pocket to put stuff, does not mean you have to put anything in there.

I have yet to discover a functional use for the middle console other than storing garbage, clutter, and change. I call my console the clutter pit. To transform the console from a stuff keeper to a clutter fighter, place a brown paper lunch bag inside to collect small trash such as receipts and candy wrappers. Designate it as a mini garbage pail to prevent junk and papers from littering the seats and floors.

Use ashtrays to hold spare change. These automotive piggy banks offer quick access to dollars and coins when approaching tolls or grabbing a quick drink at the convenience store.

What clutter fills the trunk? Check for things such as clothes, food, books, toys, and trash. The trunk is not a second closet for our oversized wardrobe nor is it an extra pantry for our huge stockpile of non-perishables. It's not a bookcase, toy chest, or garbage pail either. Make a habit of maintaining a clear trunk, with the exception of a few necessary items. Decide what is okay for the trunk—such as a first aid kit, an extra blanket, a flashlight, tire gauge, jumper cables, and windshield wiper fluid. While you're in the trunk, make sure the spare tire has air and is in usable condition.

Clean the Inside of the Car

Having no idea how to clean a car, I called on the experts with professional experience in detailing automobiles. They set me straight about the right way to clean our cars:

1. Vacuum interior, including seats, cup holders, ashtrays, and floor mats. (I never would have thought of vacuuming ashtrays and cup holders!) Remove the floor mats and vacuum the floor. For stubborn spills, dirt, and stains, use an automotive upholstery and carpet cleaning product.

2. Clean and protect inside surfaces, including vinyl, leather, and plastic, with an interior detailing cleaner. Simply spray on a dusting cloth and wipe.

3. Clean the windows using an ammonia safe window cleaner. This will prevent damaging any of the window tinting that may be on your car.

Clean the Outside of the Car

I've taken part in fundraisers where a bunch of us hosed down cars with some soapy water, but I never actually cleaned the outside—or inside—of a car on my own. Deciding that I needed to learn how, I again consulted the experts:

1. Clean the outside of the car using an automotive car wash soap. With a high quality wash mitt, get the car good and sudsy. Start from the top and move down to the bottom. Rinse thoroughly.

   • Do not use dish soap as it is harsh on paint and strips wax protection.

   • Use a dedicated wash mitt or wheel brush to clean your wheels. You do not want to contaminate your regular wash mitt with any scratchy particles from your tires that could scratch the paint the next time you wash your car.

2. Towel dry with a quality cotton terrycloth or microfiber drying towel.

3. Go over the outside of the windows with ammonia-free window cleaner.

Give the Car a Second Look—Inside and Out

Did you miss anything? Make last minute touch-ups and call it good.

If you really want to impress the neighbors (or your spouse) you can wax the car and shine the wheels. Sound like a lot of work? Surprisingly, it's not.

Easy waxing: I always pictured waxing a car to be a major task. In my mind, it compared to polishing fingernails—something that needs to be done very carefully with extra time set aside for drying—except that a car is way larger than a fingernail, so I figured waxing a car would be an all-day chore. Who knew you could wax a car in less than thirty minutes with a spray wax that you wipe like window cleaner!

Want to try waxing your car? Apply a coat of wax protection using a spray on and wipe-off aerosol wax. This type of spray wax not only makes the car look much better, but it helps protect the paint from nature's elements.

Shining tires: Do you know the secret of cleaning tires: Spray on the protectant cleaner and walk away. That's it! It's easier than using hairspray. We need more cleaning agents like this. These spray-on-and-walk-away products leave tires looking shiny and new.

Who knew cleaning a car could be so much fun? And even more enjoyable is driving a clean car!

OUTSIDE DE-CLUTTERING

The outside of our homes reflect on us. They contribute to the overall look and feel of our homes.

How do you think of your front lawn, driveway, and entrance? Realtors refer to it as curb appeal. My husband calls it prime storage area for anything that won't fit in the garage. I compare it to the wrapping paper covering a special gift—a nice looking outside makes what's inside appear even more beautiful.

Let's assess the outside of our homes. Consider these questions:

- How does your yard look? Is your garden full of weeds? Is the grass brown and fading? Could your lawn be mistaken for a field of tall grass?
- Is the paint on your house chipped or fading? Does moss grow on your shingles? Is your siding in disrepair?
- Do you keep several trash cans in plain sight? Does trash litter your driveway?
- Is your fencing and trim warping or coming apart? Are your metal railings and fences covered with rust?
- Is your front porch hidden by a jungle of foliage? Or is it a gathering place for dead plants?

Here are three simple steps for de-cluttering your lawn the quick way:

1. *Pick up debris.* Take lawn litter directly to the trash.
2. *Send displaced items home.* Bikes go back in the garage, indoor toys back in the house, and so forth.
3. *Mow the yard.* Even if you don't rake the mowings, your lawn will still look better than a field of high grass.

Since we probably have enough trouble keeping the inside of our homes looking nice, we don't want to add extra work to clean and maintain the outside. What can you do to make your outside easier to manage?

We gave up gardening. Though it's not as if we ever really started it in the first place.

My husband and I love roses. We planted three rose bushes which bloomed cascades of beautiful flowers. That was with the first buds. One thing you should realize about rose bushes is that they require constant attention. We didn't know this. And so without proper pruning, these magnificent beauties turned into overgrown, weed-ridden clutter. One day, I hope to grow a garden and maybe even give roses another try, but I will wait for the right season of my life.

Think "simplify" and give up that which causes extra work or adds clutter.

DESIGN IT CLEAN

Keeping a clean house is not just about de-cluttering and organizing. To a certain extent, how you design and decorate each room adds or subtracts to the intensity of housework. This is one lesson I wish I had learned sooner.

After de-cluttering my kitchen, I decided to buy a new table. The one I bought had beautiful carvings around the edge. Let me tell you, it was a pain to clean. When repainting my house, I selected a flat paint because it was cheaper. The cheaper paint rubbed right off every time I tried to clean the saliva our St. Bernard splashed all over the walls. And the list goes on. Learn from my mistakes. When remodeling and redecorating your home, remember to consider the following:

- Open bowl-style lighting catches bugs and moths. Cleaning out the dead insects adds to your chore list when you clean these types of lights.
- Chandeliers are nice to look at, but not so wonderful to clean. Taking down every crystal and individually polishing each one requires a lot of time.
- Furniture with lots of tiny crevices holds dirt tighter than a plain surface, thus requiring more elbow grease to keep clean.
- Furniture in different colors and styles gives the appearance of a cluttered home.
- Big furniture or too much furniture makes a room look cluttered.
- Sofa sets with patterns make an already cluttered room appear messier.
- Flat paint is not as easy to clean as satin paint. Flat paint rubs off when scrubbing off dirt and wall marks *unless* a special type of sponge is used.
- Electric stoves with flat surfaces are easier to clean than stoves with burner plates.
- Fancy doorknobs on kitchen cabinets require more work than plain doorknobs.
- Kitchen cabinets that go all the way to the ceiling prevent the tops from being used as shelves—which eventually collect a thick layer of grease from cooking.
- Tiles on counters, floors, and tubs, mean extra work cleaning the grout.
- Faucets with knobs for hot and cold require more cleaning than a lever-style faucet. Placing faucets one inch away from the wall offers just enough space to facilitate cleaning those hard to reach areas between the faucet and the wall.
- A shower curtain is easier to wash than all the crevices in a track for shower doors.

- Blinds and jalousie doors (the kind with all the slats in them) are a pain to clean. Replace them with something simpler.
- Bulky curtains are more difficult to take down and more expensive to get cleaned. Curtains that require hooks for hanging are time consuming to re-hang. The loop style provides a quicker and easier setup.
- Unfinished rooms feel cluttered. Drywall garages, attics, basements, and other unfinished areas in the house.
- Cement dust is just another thing to sweep. Seal cement floors to prevent the extra work.

INEXPENSIVE TOUCHES

Remodeling and redecorating usually means spending a lot of money. When you don't have thousands of dollars in the budget to redo your home into a low-maintenance, easy-to-clean oasis, you can still add some inexpensive touches. As you de-clutter, allocate a little money each month for the little things while tucking a few dollars away for the bigger things. Here are a few small touches you can add to your home without taking out a second mortgage:

1. Paint a fresh coat of color on living room walls.
2. Purchase quality mats. Untold amounts of dirt and debris enter the home on the soles of shoes. It will lengthen the life of your carpet, save money on vacuum bags, and make less work. Place one on each side of entryway doors, including the garage.
3. Re-caulk areas in the kitchen and bathroom where the caulking is discolored or lose.
4. Buy a new bathroom curtain to coordinate with your existing colors. Select a designer style to replace a plastic curtain. In the overall scheme of things, a pricier curtain is still inexpensive. Don't forget to purchase some matching towels too.
5. Read *Make Your House Do the Housework* by Don Aslett and Laura A. Simons (Betterway Books; 1995) for a comprehensive review of how to design a home with easy-to-clean fixtures and

materials. The book was written years ago, but it's a classic that contains time-tested ideas.

SOMETHING TO THINK ABOUT

- Where are some of the clutter hotspots in your home? What items are most often left out where they don't belong? How can you organize your stuff so that it's easy to take out and put away?
- What steps will you take to intentionally design and decorate your rooms in ways that minimize cleaning?
- Do you use your car as a mobile storage container? What boundaries do you need to establish to prevent your car from looking cluttered?
- Does the outside of your home look appealing? What can you do to make it more attractive?
- What projects or hobbies are you willing to give up to free yourself from unnecessary work?

HOMEBUILDING

I know what it is to be in need, and I know what it is to have plenty. I have learned the secret of being content in any and every situation, whether well fed or hungry, whether living in plenty or in want. I can do everything through Him who gives me strength. —*Philippians 4:12-13*

Contentment. This is the secret weapon in battling the world of marketing that tells us more is not enough. In times of abundance, be thankful. In times of need, trust in the Lord. But always embrace an attitude of contentment.

Remember to call upon the One who strengthens our souls. When we feel overwhelmed and doubt our ability to achieve presentable homes, call on God. Stand firm in the confidence that we can do all things and endure all things through Christ.

8 THE CLEAN DREAM

MY sister's house was once under siege by toys. After making major strides in de-cluttering her home, friends and family expressed delight in the progress she made. But they also uttered a few comments hinting she still had a ways to go. Here's a few of them that she shared with me:

"You did a great job picking up all the toys, Pam. But, you know, it wouldn't hurt to take out the vacuum now that the floor is clear."

"Wow! Look at this kitchen! I can see you've been working hard. Maybe you could get out the Clorox Cleanup and wipe down the counters too!"

"Where did all the clutter on the kitchen table go? I'm so proud of you. Oh look, you forgot to take a rag and actually clean the table."

Funny that none of these people offered to help my sister with the cleaning after she de-cluttered, but such is life. It was a needed wake-up call to point out that the job isn't finished when the de-cluttering is done.

When I asked my sister how she missed vacuuming the floor, wiping the counters, and cleaning the table, she explained that she didn't see that dirt. After living for so long in a messy home, clearing out all the junk made it appear like a palace to her. When I left for college, my sister still had another decade of living in a house that would continue to grow messier. She, too, struggled with keeping a clean house.

My sister explains, "To me, extreme mess is normal. That is what I grew up with. When I pick up all the clutter, it looks clean to me." This story prompts the questions, "How do you know when your home is clean?" and "How clean is clean enough?"

When I first began my quest for a clean home, I asked my friends who kept beautiful homes to share their secrets. What formula did they use? Did they hire maids? How often did they clean? But I was disappointed in the answers. They generally responded, "I clean when my house needs to be cleaned." What kind of answer is that? That's not helpful! So the conversation continued:

"How do you know when something needs to be cleaned?"

"When it's dirty."

"But don't you keep some sort of schedule?"

"Not really."

I was getting nowhere fast. "Then tell me how often you vacuum."

"Once a day or maybe every couple days. It depends on what the carpet looks like."

"What about sweeping and mopping the kitchen floor?"

"I probably sweep once a day and mop once a week, but I do it more often if the floors need it."

Aha. Maybe I was onto something. "So you do keep a schedule!"

"I don't call it a schedule. I see that something needs to be cleaned and I clean it."

When I asked my friends about cleaning, a pattern emerged that indicated there was a schedule, but they refused to acknowledge using one. They claimed they didn't use any special system, but I later learned they did have a system—based on standards. They each went by a personal definition of clean. When that definition wasn't met, it was time to clean.

It took me a long time to comprehend this. Everything I read told me I needed some kind of system that involved scheduling housework. Many books recommended writing my chores on 3x5 cards. That didn't work because my index cards got lost in the clutter. Then there was zone cleaning, but that was just too difficult to follow for my simple mind. Other books suggested cleaning fifteen minutes a day. That would be wonderful if my home was reasonably clean to begin with. Sure I could maintain my messy home with a few minutes of housework each day, but how could I do better?

Nothing seemed to work for me. When I tried cleaning only when something looked dirty, I failed miserably. I missed areas or forgot entire sections. Overwhelmed by all the catch-up work necessary to make the house appear tidy, I felt defeated.

Establishing a schedule sounded a little easier. I liked the idea of using a checklist to remind me what chores needed to be done. But if something wasn't on the schedule, it stayed dirty. And with all the de-cluttering yet to be done, I couldn't keep up with the list of chores.

The marriage of cleaning by standards and cleaning by schedule provided the ultimate solution. I decided what my standards of clean look like. Once I defined specific standards, they became my goals. I knew I couldn't achieve my vision of clean in a day, especially with all the de-cluttering yet to be done, so I set up a schedule of daily, weekly, monthly, and annual chores. The schedule is more like a checklist. I do what I can and start fresh the next day. I call this combination of standards and schedule my cleaning plan.

What are your standards of clean? Determine what is acceptable and write it down. Is a soap ring by the sink okay until you get to it on your schedule? Can you live with fingerprints on the fridge? How much grease can you handle on the hood over the stove?

Have you developed a cleaning routine? Do you know what chores need to be completed daily and which ones are okay to skip if you don't get to them? Write a chore list and decide how often each one needs to be performed. When you notice something doesn't meet your definition of clean, take care of it—*even if it is not on the schedule.*

Think about how specific you want to get. Many of the routines I initially tried to implement were too general, like "clean the bathroom." But what does it really mean to clean the bathroom? Is it just cleaning the toilet? Or is it mopping the floor, wiping the counters, and scrubbing the tub? And do I have to do all of that each day?

To create a cleaning plan, write it out so that a child could look at it and know what needs to be done. When something on your cleaning plan doesn't work any longer, change it around.

I discovered grouping similar weekly chores together works better for me than zone cleaning. For example, all switch plates get wiped on a certain day rather than those in just one room.

I keep a checklist—a list of daily chores makes me feel a sense of accomplishment when I cross them out.

Use my plan as a template to develop your own system. Feel free to modify this to fit your cleaning needs. If you own live plants, add watering plants to the list. If you have pets, especially ones that shed, some of the weekly chores may need to be moved to daily chores.

Daily Chores

Divide the items on the list below into a morning and evening cleaning routine. Customize this to your household needs:

- Make the bed.
- Feed pets.
- Wash the dishes. Clean the kitchen sink, including the faucet. (If it means plates will stack up in the sink just because there's space for a few more glasses, then don't wait until the dishwasher is completely full.)
- Clear new clutter off countertops and tables.
- Wipe countertops and tables.
- Sweep the kitchen floor.
- Clean the toilet, inside and out.
- Clear new clutter on bathroom counters. Clean the sink, including faucet.
- Pick up clothes on bathroom floor and do a quick wipe-down of the floor with a paper towel.
- Do a minimum of one load of laundry. (This includes emptying the dryer, folding clothes, putting them away, and cleaning the lint filter for the next load.)

- Check wastebaskets, take out trash if three-quarters full or more.
- Set out next day's clothes.
- Take a "trash walk." Stroll around the house with an empty grocery bag in hand, looking for debris that needs to be picked up.
- Take a "clutter walk." Stroll around the house looking for things that are out of place and take them back to their rightful homes.
- Remedy anything that does not meet your standards of clean as you come across it.

Weekly Chores

Day 1
- Mop floors and vacuum carpets.
- Clean mats and throw rugs.

Day 2
- Change bed linens.
- De-clutter purse.

Day 3
- Clean outsides of appliances.
- Clean mirrors.
- Scour tub.

Day 4
- Clean doorknobs and door handles.
- Clean switch plates.
- Clean telephones, computers, remote controls, and other heavily used devices.

Day 5
- Brush animals.
- Perform "quick clean" of car (five or so minutes of de-cluttering).
- Empty all the trash. (Assign this chore for the eve of your regularly scheduled trash pickup day.) Place a few extra bags in the

bottom of wastebaskets so that a fresh bag is available when you empty the trash during the week.

Day 6

• Work on monthly chores.

Monthly Chores

Week 1

• Clean the inside of the refrigerator, microwave, stove (and stove hood), and other appliances.

• Wash out wastebaskets.

• Clean outside of cabinets.

• Clean under the kitchen and bathroom sinks.

Week 2

• Clean baseboards.

• Clear clutter from tops of washer and dryer, then wipe tops of washer and dryer.

• Pull out appliances and furniture to clean under and behind them with mop or vacuum.

• Clean under beds.

Week 3

• Clean windows and inside window panes.

• Check walls and doors for scuff marks and clean where needed.

• Dust furniture and figurines and other knickknacks.

• Dust light fixtures.

Week 4

• Groom pets.

• Check cabinets, drawers, and closets for new clutter and straighten them. Wash tray or basket where silverware is kept.

• Superclean car (see chapter 7).

Annual Chores

Fit these in throughout the year or in one big burst during Spring cleaning season:

- Call professional cleaners to steam clean carpets and furniture, letting them clean the air ducts as well. Pay the extra few dollars for a Teflon coat on the carpet—it is well worth it.
- Clean drapes and curtains.
- Clean coils under refrigerator.
- Clean garage and other major storage areas such as spare rooms, attics, and basements.
- Thin out filing cabinets, pulling out papers that are no longer necessary to keep.
- Perform a room-by-room de-cluttering spree, doing a different room each month.

If something is already clean when you get to it on your list, skip it. If there's nothing in the trash, would you take out an empty bag? No. So why wash the windows when they look great to begin with?

Be smart when deciding if you can hold off on a chore until the next time around. Places such as kitchens and bathrooms still harbor bacteria even when they look clean. Bedding may appear fresh, but then again you can't see those microscopic mites.

Don't sweat it if you don't follow your cleaning plan to a tee. If you never had one before, it may take a while to establish new habits. Focus on what you're able to do rather than what you missed. Incorporate an amount of chores you can handle while de-cluttering. Add a little more each week.

Think of learning how to keep a clean house as an infant learning to walk. It takes about a year for babies to develop leg muscles strong enough for them to stand on their own. It takes time for cleaning habits to become ingrained in our daily routine.

When children stand by themselves for the first time, we cheer them on. When they tumble while trying to take those first steps, we encourage them to keep going. And before we know it, little feet scamper all over the house, running every which way as if they had been walking forever. Learning to keep a clean home is similar. In the beginning, you may need someone to hold your hand. When people encourage us, they motivate us to take another step. Sometimes we tumble, but we get back up and keep trying.

Set a goal for yourself. Every day do one thing to make your house look a little nicer than it looked the day before. Take small baby steps. Seek progress, not perfection.

HOME CLEANING SUMMIT

It will be easier to maintain a presentable home when you get the whole family onboard. Decide cleaning and de-cluttering expectations as a family. Individuals take ownership in this process by being given a voice. Ask each family member:

- What do you want the house to look like?
- What are you willing to do to reach and maintain that vision?
- What standards of clean would you like to define for our home?

Use this time to create a cleaning schedule and chore chart. Select a date to evaluate the effectiveness of your family's housekeeping efforts. Consider holding monthly summits to discuss cleaning and de-cluttering issues.

In my household, we have weekly family conferences during which we discuss our schedules, current projects, and things we'd like to do. We incorporate an informal version of a home cleaning summit into these meetings.

We also do ten minutes of daily couch time together. During these mini-meetings we share what we did during the day (not just what we cleaned), remind one another of the evening's schedule, and ask for help with anything that still needs to get done. This is our time to touch base with one another and take the family pulse.

Think about how you can meet with your family to discuss what's on your mind while giving others a chance to say their piece. Homemaking is not just about keeping a clean house. As home managers we need to communicate with the family. We need to practice dialogues, not monologues. Family time creates incredible opportunities to bring your spouse and children together as a team to make a beautiful home together.

When we get out of the habit of meeting, I notice my family has a more difficult time with the upkeep of the home. Consider scheduling weekly family meetings and make them a priority.

The apostle Paul may not have had cluttered homes in mind when he wrote in Hebrews 10:25, "Let us not give up meeting together, as some are in the habit of doing, but let us encourage one another—and all the more as you see the Day approaching." However, this verse serves as a reminder to me that I need to meet with my family so we can encourage one another in all of our goals.

DE-CLUTTERING STRATEGIES

As you talk with your family to discuss ways to simplify your home by living with less, brainstorm creative strategies to make de-cluttering fun. I call my favorite strategy *sacred cow hunting*. I like it because it forces me to re-think why I keep the things I keep. Evaluate the ideas below and decide if you want to incorporate any of these techniques in your battle against clutter.

SACRED COW HUNTING

In the business world, a *sacred cow* refers to an outdated practice that inhibits positive change. In homemaking, sacred cows prevent the transformation of our messy houses into presentable homes. They're the items we keep due to faulty thinking. We tell ourselves, *That's the way we've always done it*, or *That's something we've always owned*.

Go on a sacred cow hunt. Look for things you normally wouldn't consider parting with. Evaluate if these prized possessions are truly worth keeping.

Ask questions such as:

- What was the original reason for obtaining this item?
- Why am I keeping the item?
- Is this item still used for its intended purpose? Why or why not?
- Do I enjoy using it? Why or why not?

- Do I treat this item in a respectful manner? How does the way I store or display it show that I value it?
- What would happen if I threw it away?
- How do I feel about keeping it?

Based on your answers, objectively decide what you want to do with the item.

Practice sacred cow hunting with me. Let's look at holiday storage. Hmmm . . . I see a Christmas tree. I certainly can't part with that, right? Let's ask the questions anyway.

- *What was the original reason for buying my Christmas tree?* So I could use it to celebrate Christmas.
- *Why am I keeping this?* Because it is a tradition in my family to celebrate Christmas with a tree. I like that it makes my house look festive during the holidays.
- *Is the tree still used for its intended purpose? Why or why not?* Yes. I put it up every year because I own it. Owning it obligates me to use it. Plus, that's the way we've always celebrated Christmas.
- *Do I enjoy using it? Why or why not?* Putting up the tree and taking it down has become a burden. I no longer enjoy this because no one else is interested in helping me with it. I dislike taking off ornaments, putting them back in their boxes, and storing them for another year. I still enjoy putting presents under the tree and relaxing to soft Christmas music in a dim room lit by tree lights.
- *Do I treat this item in a respectful manner?* How does the way I display or store it show that I value it? I take the time to decorate the tree to make it look pleasing. I pack the tree back in its box. I haphazardly toss ornaments, lights, and other decorations into a storage box.
- *What would happen if I threw the tree away and celebrated without a tree?* If I didn't have a tree, I wouldn't have to spend time putting it up, decorating it, and taking it down. Without the tree, I can lose the extra Christmas lights, ornaments, garland, and ribbon. No tree means fewer decorations, less clutter, and less

stuff to store. I can still celebrate Christmas with a real tree or even a potted miniature pine.

• *How do I feel about keeping it?* Based on my answers, I will no longer keep an artificial tree and most of the decorations that go along with it. Instead, I will try a new tradition of celebrating Christmas with a real tree. If I discover that a real tree is too much work or that I like the artificial tree better, I can always buy a new one during those 75-percent-off sales after Christmas. I will keep only the decorations I absolutely love.

The above Sacred Cow Hunt actually happened in my home. I love not having to bother with an artificial tree!

CLEAN SWEEP HOME EDITION

Did you ever watch the show "Clean Sweep" on The Learning Channel (TLC)? Why not perform your own modified version of the show?

Mimic TLC's famous program without the cameras, personal carpenters, designers, and professional organizers. Get a team of friends to help you move everything out of one or two rooms in your house. Create a *keep pile*, a *toss pile*, and a *sale pile*.

Do a quick twenty-minute sort of everything. Move as much as you can into either the sale pile or toss pile. Any questionable items go in the keep pile to evaluate during the major sort.

Perform the major sort, establishing a new keep pile. Be conscientious of the room size and what will reasonably fit back in there.

Hold a big yard sale. Price the items to sell. Anything not sold, goes *immediately* to a local charity. No storing things in the garage for another yard sale next week.

I performed a clean sweep like this at my sister's house. She had a sunroom, basement, and garage, all full of storage. People asked us if we were moving because it looked as if everything she owned was in the front yard—extra furniture, decorations, dishes, books, toys, clothes, you name it. We priced things to sell and made a modest profit. But the best part was all the extra space this created in her house.

FREEBIE GIVEAWAY

Instead of a lawn sale, have a freebie giveaway. Tell people they must take items by the box. No picking through things. Later, they can donate or sell what they don't want.

This is one that I love to do. You can get rid of a lot in a short period of time. When I did the big yard sale with my sister, we had a huge freebie pile filled with things that would not fetch a decent price. When the yard sale ended, everything went to the freebie pile. People looking for free stuff saved us the trouble of making several trips to haul away leftovers to a donation center.

CLUTTERSIZE

Ever heard of Jazzersize—exercising using Jazz moves to music? Well, cluttersizing is exercise by de-cluttering to music. Find a favorite adrenaline-pumping CD. Play it while de-cluttering. This works best when working with friends.

HOME REPO STORE

Not sure what to do with all the stuff lying around the house belonging to other family members? Create a Home Repo store! Put other people's belongings in a box to be "sold" once a week or once a month. Select specific hours to open the Home Repo store. Family members are responsible for reclaiming their repossessed items. Offer the owners their belongings for sale at a flat rate of 25 cents or even $1.00. If they choose not to come get them, they lose them. Be gracious, lest you find family members adding your stuff to your home repo store.

Modify the store guidelines to fit your needs. When I did this with my husband, we didn't charge each other to get things back. We used it as a tool to discipline ourselves to pick up our stuff in a timely manner.

DE-CLUTTERING OLYMPICS

One of the questions I frequently hear when I give de-cluttering workshops is how to get kids motivated to clean. Most children and adults have a competitive nature. Why not bring out some competition for cleaning the house?

Set aside a weekend for your own De-cluttering Olympics. All family members must participate. Offer prizes for different categories such as cleanest room, most items tossed, fastest de-clutterer, and outstanding sportsmanship (for helping other family members clean and de-clutter).

To make it fun for all participants, create an award category for everyone. Choose prizes that will not add clutter to the home. Take children to their favorite restaurant, a family arcade, or maybe miniature golfing. Give older kids gift certificates to a movie or tickets to a sporting event. Treat your spouse to a massage or a special dinner—or offer verbal praise.

CLEANING PARTY

Some people host tea parties, others throw painting parties and moving parties. Why not a cleaning party? Invite a few friends over to help with the cleaning. Keep plenty of beverages on hand, including bottled water. Have snacks available—the kind that won't make a lot of crumbs.

When I fall behind on the housekeeping, having a few gal pals over to help always energizes me. Sometimes, they just visit while I clean. All they need to do is sit at the kitchen table and chat with me while I superclean the fridge or mop the floor.

THE MINIMIZER

Look for collections around the house and think of ways to shrink them. My husband minimized his tool collection by selling some of the bulky ones and replacing them with newer, slimmer, all-purpose versions. Here are some more ideas:

- Take pictures of all those trophies from Little League. Put the photos in a scrapbook and toss the trophies.
- Not ready to part with a T-shirt collection styling clever sayings? Hire someone to make them into a quilt.
- Remove patches from old scouting uniforms. Get rid of the uniforms and use the patches to make a shadowbox.

GENERAL CONTRACTOR

Hire professionals to help you create the look you desire. Employ a cleaning lady to assist in scrubbing down the house. Call a professional organizer to help you with sorting and organizing. Consult with an interior designer for decorating your home.

About once a year, I treat myself to a cleaning lady. It's just nice to have a break now and then. Depending on our finances, I decide if I want to sub-contract everything or just the least appealing chores.

KRIS KRINGLE

Remember back in school being someone's secret gift-giver? Play Kris Kringle as an adult by re-gifting brand-new items that are cluttering the home. But don't wait for Christmas. Let the season of goodwill begin today!

Give items to your church ministries—they make great giveaways for special events. Surprise a new mom by giving her the baby clothes your little one never wore. Give a book you're not interested in to a friend who will love it.

TOP TEN LIST

Scavenge the house for the Top Ten Clutter Collection Spots. Every family member participates by creating his or her own list. Meet together and compare what each person found. Collection spots that everyone noticed become the priority clutter hotspots to be worked on that day. The following day, each family member creates another list, the top ten spots where progress was made. This gives everyone the opportunity to give encouragement and receive positive feedback.

I like doing top ten lists because they help me prioritize where to focus my attention. When my husband makes these lists with me, I know we are on the same page. We don't feel as if we're nagging each other because together we evaluate areas in which to focus our decluttering efforts.

SOMETHING TO THINK ABOUT

- What cleaning methods have you tried in the past? From previous experience, what worked and what didn't work?
- What chore do you like least? Have you tried using a cleaning buddy, playing music, or testing different cleaning supplies? How can you make it more enjoyable? What chore do you like the most? Why?
- What are some of the sacred cows in your home? How would it impact your workload if you parted with them?
- What are some of the collections you can reduce in size? How might you go about minimizing them?
- In what ways can you make de-cluttering more fun? How might your family like to participate?

HOMEBUILDING

Consider it pure joy, my brothers, whenever you face trials of many kinds, because you know that the testing of your faith develops perseverance. Perseverance must finish its work so that you may be mature and complete, not lacking anything. —James 1:2-4

We may not think of housework as pure joy, but why not give it a try? Develop a positive attitude because Christ is at work within us. Just as our homes are a work in progress, so are we.

9 INVISIBLE CLUTTER

CLUTTER goes beyond those things that invade our homes. It comes in different forms that steal space in our minds and hearts.

Let's think about this. Physical clutter is what the name implies, the stuff around us that we can see and touch. My clutterbug friend Katie describes the look of physical clutter in her home, "Every time I walk through the front door, the first thought that runs through my mind is 'Oh, no! We've been robbed!'" Really, it's just too much stuff lying around on her living room floor.

Sometimes we think of physical clutter as invisible when we hide our junk in drawers and closets. Since we don't see it, it's not there. But it really is there. All we need to do is open the drawer or closet door.

One could even call the toxins in the air we breathe and the food we eat another form of clutter. These toxins attack us on a cellular level but impact our health in a big way. I notice a difference when I use scented laundry detergent instead of the "free and clear" type. Eating certain kinds of food results in stomach pain and severe fatigue. This type of microscopic clutter may be invisible to the human eye, but we can make choices that minimize its impact on us.

However, as we de-clutter our homes, we need to be aware of the *real* invisible clutter that invades our hearts and minds. It comes in the form of busyness, gossip, worry, unhealthy relationships, stress, discontentment, anger, and other negative emotions.

ACTIVITY CLUTTER

It's hard to keep a clean house when we lead such busy lives. With the advent of super-sized meals, we also embraced super-sized calendars. But no matter how large the calendar we purchase, there are still only twenty-four hours in one day.

If you want to de-clutter your home, you must de-clutter your calendar. Examine the number of activities that fill your week:

- It's good to pursue your interests, but not to the neglect of your home and family. Participating in crafters club, aerobics classes, moms' group, book club, and Bible study—while volunteering at the soup kitchen, serving on the prayer team, playing in the city softball league, and taking graduate level college courses may be just a little too much.

- It's a noble act to lead a small group study or volunteer in a leadership capacity at church. But if you are unable to minister to your family because you spend so much time ministering to others, then it's time to re-evaluate if you should continue in your leadership role. Sometimes only one activity is too much depending on how much it requires of you.

- It's admirable that you want to expose your kids to soccer, baseball, 4-H, scouting, piano lessons, voice lessons, drama team, and karate, but do you have to do it all at once? Don't neglect yourself and your home by spending so much time chauffeuring your kids around to their activities; and stop encouraging your children to embrace overload. A good rule of thumb is no more than two activities per child at any one time. Don't forget to count church youth group as an activity. That leaves only *one* other opening. If you have several children, look for activities they can do together.

How does calendar overload affect you? Do you complain that you're too tired to keep up with your household chores? Do you attribute the mess to not having the time to clean?

As I work to find the right balance, it helps to simplify my schedule. Otherwise, it's too easy for the busyness of life to distract me from the new clutter that invades my home. Mail piles up; a couple dirty plates in the sink become twenty dishes. Toys don't get put away. Laundry baskets overflow with clothes waiting to be washed.

☐ ☐ ☐

Activity clutter affects more than our ability to maintain a presentable home. We miss out on our families because of the activities that demand our attention. Self-care becomes less of a priority.

Too many activities also impact our spiritual growth. How does calendar clutter affect your relationship with God? Do you find yourself too tired to pray? Do you skip church because you're too exhausted to do much of anything when the weekend rolls around?

When my schedule is overloaded with commitments, I'm more likely to eat fast food that clutters my body with empty calories. I forget to take my prescription. I have less energy to invest in relationships. I make poor, impulsive decisions rather than thinking through my options and their potential outcomes. Going to church becomes a chore rather than something I look forward to. And when I'm overloaded with busyness, I tend to buy more stuff.

THE GIFT OF TIME

What weapon helps defeat activity clutter? Margin. What does margin look like? In this book, it's the white space on the edges of the pages. Imagine what it would look like to read this or any other book if the words start at the very top left-hand corner and keep going to the bottom right-hand corner. Every time you turn the page, it looks the same. There's no space for your eyes to rest.

When I read, I sometimes take notes. I'll write a question or comment in the margin. But in the book with no white space, there's no place to write my comments.

When you live with no margin, there's no resting space. There's no room to meditate on life, no time to make thoughtful comments or pose meaningful questions. All you do is move from one activity to the next.

Adding margin to your life means giving yourself *the gift of time.* When you give yourself the gift of time, you can take care of chores that didn't get done during their scheduled times or run unexpected errands. If you fall ill, it will be easier to catch up on housework once you feel better. You feel less stress. You don't feel overwhelmed from having too much to do in short periods of time.

Add margin to your life. Leave earlier for work so you don't have to rush. Allocate extra time for the drive to school in case of a traffic jam. When given a deadline for a work project, self-impose an earlier deadline. Allow for additional time when eating meals to savor the taste and enjoy the company of loved ones at the dinner table. When planning for business or personal engagements, block out extra time past their scheduled ending times in case they run late. Plan to arrive fifteen minutes early, and bring something to do to fill the time gap such as a book to read or a crossword to solve—it's more relaxing than rushing and worrying about being late.

Here are a few ways to help you embrace margin: practice Sabbath rest, create a time budget, and establish calendar boundaries.

Practice Sabbath rest. Start by looking to God for answers. Look at His example. He worked for six days on His creation and rested on the seventh. Designate one day each week as a day of rest. Getting up early on a Sunday morning to go to church is not restful to me, so I choose Saturday as my day of Sabbath rest. I try to spend my Sabbath at home. As I do personal study on this concept, I refine how I apply it to my life. For example, I learned the Sabbath doesn't just come and then I get to rest. It requires preparation to experience true Sabbath rest. Thoughtful planning for Sabbath makes me more intentional about setting aside time to refresh my soul.

Think about what an ideal Sabbath looks like to you. Consider how God would want you to celebrate the gift of Sabbath. Do you light candles? Or break open the China cabinet and set out your best silverware? Do you refrain from cooking or shopping? Do you abstain from television or other technology? Or maybe you spend time outdoors where you can experience nature and marvel at God's creation?

God gave us the Sabbath for a reason. It's so important that it's described in the Bible as both a command and a gift.

As you incorporate Sabbath into your calendar, activity clutter will automatically decrease. When you practice Sabbath rest, you will be giving up other commitments and building a natural boundary to defend your time.

Create a time budget. How do you invest your time? How many hours each day do you allocate to sleeping, working, commuting, hanging out with friends, visiting with family, watching television, eating, cleaning, and other activities?

First, assess where you spend your time. Take a sheet of lined paper. Write the days of the week across the top of the page. Write the time in 30-minute increments along the left-hand margin starting from the time your alarm clock rings in the morning. Plug in all your commitments first. Don't forget to include time for commuting—label it "drive." Next, add breakfast, lunch, and dinner. Mark the time you spend getting ready for the day, running errands, exercising, buying groceries, cleaning the house, and engaging in other activities with terms that work for you.

Where can you add margin? If the commute to work or school is fifteen minutes, then mark it for thirty minutes. Place a large X in the time blocks that you want to keep free from *ongoing* commitments.

Share your time budget with your family. Communicate to your family what you expect of them. Should you institute a family dinner hour, do household members understand that the phone is off limits? Do they know that dinner does not officially end until the table is cleared, leftovers put away, the table and stove wiped down, pots and pans scrubbed clean, and dishes placed in the dishwasher?

If you need to schedule a block of alone time on the weekend, what does that look like? Does your husband know not to call you to the garage to hold a piece of wood as he saws it in two? Do your children know that you need some uninterrupted time and to bother you only in case of emergency? Do they understand that a misplaced toy does not constitute an emergency?

Evaluate your time budget. Talk to your family about their time budgets. What do you want to change? How do others feel about it? What does your ideal schedule look like? Play around with it and work toward a schedule that reflects your values, passions, and priorities.

Establish calendar boundaries. Defend your calendar from activity clutter by setting guidelines on how you will spend your time and why. There are many opportunities out there—places to go, people to see, things to do that are more fun than tending to our homes and loved ones.

I defend my calendar by protecting our family time in the evenings. After scheduling too many events after the family dinner hour, I realized how important it is for us to spend this time at home. It felt as if we were always on the go. I woke up every morning just as exhausted as when I fell asleep. How could I keep a presentable home when I was never there to clean it? And when I was home, I was too tired to give our home any attention.

We've forgotten the significance of the evening hours. It used to be the time that families rested and relaxed together. Back in the day, one person washed the dishes while the other dried them. Messes were cleaned up together. There was no rushing to an activity every night of the week. Now, dishes remain on the table despite dishwashers that do most of the work. If there's nothing on the calendar, dirty plates still don't get cleaned because we sprint to the couch so we don't miss our favorite television show—even though we have the technology to record them. Our busyness has instilled laziness.

Do you want to join me in protecting evenings for home and family? Think through activities that call for evening commitments. Can you eliminate any of these from your schedule? Consider how your home life would differ if you spent *every* evening at home. Freeing up every evening may not be possible, but humor me with this brainstorming exercise. If you had nothing on the calendar, what would you do to fill that time at home? Would you de-clutter the spare bedroom? Finish those partially completed projects such as the paint job in the kitchen? Establish new family traditions such as a weekly game night? Break out the Bible that's collecting dust on your shelf? Or maybe just get some overdue rest from an otherwise busy day?

This is what defending our evenings looks like in practice for our family. Rather than being legalistic, my husband and I choose to be *selective*. We avoid committing to more than two evening activities per week.

Tuesday night is Scout night. This fits with our vision of saving our evenings for family time because we usually attend as a family, but sometimes my husband or I need a break and give the other the night off. Depending on our overall schedule, we might participate in a couples' small group study that provides childcare. Sometimes we choose not to be involved in a life group, but find other ways to stay connected with our church body. I also have a required teacher meeting once per month and an optional home educator monthly meeting.

I think of all the other things I could add to our evening schedule. There are women's ministry fellowship events, business and networking dinners, professional workshops, writers groups, speaking engagements, volunteer opportunities, aerobics and Pilates classes, not to mention kids' activities and the countless other potential commitments. I turn most of these down. Even if they are only once per month, these monthly activities add up. I don't want to be a slave to my calendar, and I'm guessing you don't want to be a slave to yours either.

De-clutter your calendar and make time for investing in your homes, your family, yourself, and your relationship with God.

CONVERSATIONAL CLUTTER

Who says clutter can't spew from our mouths? It comes in the forms of profanity, gossip, coarse joking, and complaining. Women, because we tend to be talkers, must watch out for conversational clutter. When we start talking we should be sure what we are saying is encouraging, uplifting, noble, and praiseworthy. Is our conversation laced with put-downs and negativity? We are told "For out of the overflow of the heart the mouth speaks" (Matthew 12:34). What do your words and tone of voice say about your heart? One of my favorite Bible verses is Ephesians. 4:29: "Do not let any unwholesome talk come out of your mouths, but only what is helpful for building others up according to their needs, that it may benefit those who listen." In my book, if our words don't meet this command, we are talking trash. And we all know that trash is another form of clutter.

INTELLECTUAL CLUTTER

Sometimes facts and trivia clutter our minds. My baby brother is a sports fanatic, memorizing stats and scores. My husband spends hours on the computer surfing sites about motorcycles. I am a Fox News junkie. What is your addiction? Are you obsessed with the stock market? Do you know the words to every song recorded by your favorite singer? Can you repeat lines from movies on cue? And what about the slogans and jingles from watching so many commercials? Beware of information overload. We don't want clutter in our homes, nor do we desire it in our minds.

RELATIONSHIP CLUTTER

Another form of clutter comes from the emotional drain of tending unhealthy relationships. Think about friends who use you to meet their needs without giving back. They're eager to take but not so eager to give. Friends like these wear you down, and time spent with them can leave you feeling depleted.

Being the helper friend that I was, I fell into this trap. Certain people in my life took a lot of mental energy when I hung out with them. Not wanting to cut myself off from these friends, I set boundaries on how much time I would visit with them each week. As I spent less time with them, my energy increased. I began to understand how negative-thinking friends impacted me on a physiological level. Conversely, I started noticing that other friends had the opposite effect. Their enthusiasm for life was contagious. They were motivating, encouraging, and uplifting. Instead of feeling tired after our time together, I felt energized.

EAGLES, TURKEYS, AND ALGAE

We have a choice when it comes to the people we choose as friends. We can fly with the eagles, trot with the turkeys, or float with the algae. Most of us don't choose algae for friends. These are the abusers and the law breakers—the bad influences and people with unhealthy boundaries who cause us unspeakable pain. But too many times we do the turkey trot rather than soar with the eagles.

One way to determine who fits in the algae category is to ask yourself, *Would I trust this person with my child?* It's not enough that the person would cause no physical harm. Also ask yourself, *How would this person impact my child's character and spiritual growth?* You can use this litmus whether or not you have children. If someone uses a litany of profanity in front of a child, it clues you into algae. If a person lacks awareness of age appropriate speech content when kids are around, it indicates that this is not a safe person to invite into your circle of friends.

Sometimes, as the saying goes, wolves come in sheep's clothing. We need to pray for discernment about who we welcome into our lives and how much of ourselves we share with them.

We all have turkeys in our lives—people content with the status quo, lacking ambition, and complaining about their troubles. They may talk about wanting to improve their lives but find excuses for why they can't move forward. They may say they have ambition, but their actions prove otherwise. Instead of brainstorming solutions to life's challenges, they prefer to play the blame game. They always find an excuse for their lot in life. So they accept it, just trotting around like turkeys.

Then there's the eagles. These are the people who live extraordinary lives. Mediocre, average, and ordinary are not good enough. They know that God made us for so much more than that. They live a life *set apart*, growing their faith in Christ in both the best of times and their darkest hours. They don't have to be millionaires or hold fancy positions in the corporate world. Nor do they have to be missionaries in Africa or clones of Mother Teresa. Regardless of their station in life, they understand that wealth can disappear in an instant and that there are more important things than money, power, and material possessions.

People who live as eagles live life to the fullest. They seek out opportunity rather than waiting for opportunity to knock. They do for themselves what others *could* do for them. Their life decisions don't depend on what their friends decide. When hard times come their way, they focus on solutions rather than dwelling on the problem. They set goals for themselves and pursue them with intensity and integrity. They live out the passions that God places in their hearts.

Who are the eagles in your life? These are the people who bring you up instead of pulling you down. They put a premium on relationships over stuff. And they tend not to add emotional clutter to your life.

Keep in mind that these are general terms meant to help you evaluate friendships that cause emotional drain. No one is stuck in a turkey box forever. And even eagles struggle with clutter and maintaining presentable homes.

If you want to minimize the relationship clutter in your life, choose friends wisely. Then establish healthy boundaries with them.

We can also experience relationship clutter from trying to maintain close friendships with too many people—no matter if we categorize them as eagles, turkeys, or algae. We only have so much of ourselves to give. We can't keep giving and giving to everybody all the time.

I want to be an eagle, how about you? But we can't soar like eagles with clutter strapped to our wings—whether it's visible or invisible.

FAMILY DYSFUNCTION

We can choose our friends, but we can't choose our family. Friends come and go, but family is forever—no matter the level of the dysfunction.

Before I continue, take note that I'm not advocating you ignore pain inflicted by toxic family members. Those types of relationship issues are beyond the scope of this book. If you experience abuse as an adult, reach out for help. If you struggle with memories of childhood abuse, seek a Christian counselor who can help you make peace with your past.

I want to make the point that even family members can add relationship clutter to our lives. For most of us, we can get past the dysfunction—we all live through some level of it. As imperfect beings in a fallen world, we all miss the mark when it comes to the perfect family. Everybody has quirks and shortcomings.

If family members act like turkeys, you can't force them to change. However, you can change your responses to them. If your Aunt Betsy wears you out from gossip, choose to spend less time with her. If your adult daughter takes advantage of you as the "babysitting grandma," stop giving her permission to do it by saying yes every time she asks you to watch the kids regardless of plans you may have had. If your brother asks you to loan him money to pay the rent, but he can still afford an expensive cell phone plan, satellite television, and the latest gaming system, tell him no.

Poor boundaries with friends and family create relationship clutter. Good boundaries build healthy relationships and happy homes.

PSYCHOLOGICAL CLUTTER

There is a psychological realm where collections of bad feelings and negative emotions dwell inside of us, cluttering our hearts. Psychological clutter is the emotional heaviness that resides in our hearts. These weights are not tangible, but nonetheless they burden our souls. What does the psychological clutter look like in your heart? Is it anxiety? Worry? Bitterness? Anger? Pride? Envy? Discontentment? Guilt? Unforgiveness?

There's no magic formula for dealing with these things. You must work it out on your own with God. If you were to focus on just one of these for today, take a look at unforgiveness.

Confess your sins. Ask God to forgive you. Open your heart to Jesus. Let that be the first step in de-cluttering your heart.

Forgive others as God forgives you. Forgiveness is a choice, not a feeling. You can choose to forgive others, no matter how horribly they behaved toward you. Sometimes forgiveness doesn't come in neat little packages. The person who wronged you may not even acknowledge what they did that hurt you. But in order to de-clutter your heart, you must extend forgiveness—even if the person who caused you pain fails to apologize. And sometimes the person you need to forgive most is you.

SOMETHING TO THINK ABOUT

- How will you eliminate activities from your calendar? Which ones will you let go?
- What does your ideal Sabbath look like?
- What relationships do you need to step back from? What boundaries do you need to implement to develop healthier relationships?
- How many other types of invisible clutter can you think of? List them all.
- Who has hurt you that you still need to forgive? Extend forgiveness to that person and take the extra step of saying a prayer of blessing on him or her.

HOMEBUILDING

Search me, O God, and know my heart; test me and know my anxious thoughts. See if there is any offensive way in me, and lead me in the way everlasting. —Psalm 139:23-24

How clean is your heart? Not one of us is perfect, so we all have a little work to do. Good thing none of our friends can give a white-glove test on our hearts. But God knows what's in there, and He wants to help with the de-cluttering.

It's been said that God makes His home in our hearts. Let's do a little heart cleaning. Let go of the invisible clutter that doesn't need to be there such as bitterness, unforgiveness, worry, and greed. Ask God to remove these things and replace them with joy, grace, trust, and contentment. Confess what needs God's forgiveness that He may create in you a cleansed heart. And as you keep a neat and clean home, make a habit of daily heart cleaning.

10 SABOTEURS OF A CLEAN HOME

WHILE fighting the clutter war and finding victory, we must be on guard for the saboteurs that threaten our clean homes.

Do you ever start cleaning your home only to be sidetracked by something else? This happens to me all the time. In fact, it happened to me as I wrote the first edition of this book. I thought, "Look at this mess! And I'm writing a book about keeping a clean house?" While working on the second edition, it's déjà vu. The irony doesn't escape me that as I devote time toward revisions, my house beckons me to clean it. But as I listen to the sound of the wash machine and dishwasher, I find comfort in the fact that my deadline will not sabotage my efforts to keep a clean home.

If I focus on my writing and nothing else, my home suffers. The Second Law of Thermodynamics—the natural tendency for things to fall into disorder—is at work. Since our homes have a natural tendency toward mess and disorder, we can't get sidetracked by other things pulling us away from our home management goals. We must prevent our other priorities, interests, and situations from sabotaging our desire to keep a presentable home.

When my son was a toddler, there were days I felt as if I was competing with my growing baby and he was winning. My boy liked to find stacks of books, papers, and pens to fling in the air, while locating special hiding places for the remote control, phone, and car keys. He enjoyed moving furniture to reach the kitchen faucet to dump pools of water on the floor. Then, when I tried to get some rest, my little monkey jumped on top of me like a rodeo cowboy yelling, "Giddyup!"

As he grew older, he discovered that laundry baskets make great "cars." He dumped the clothes out of the basket so he could hop inside and ride down the stairs in it. When I explained to him that this was not safe, he put on his bike helmet to emulate a real race car driver.

First, understand that our children are blessings, not saboteurs. They do what kids do—make messes. It's part of our job as parents to train them in the discipline of cleaning.

My circumstance as the mom of a young toddler hampered my efforts to clean. Sometimes we have control over our circumstances, and sometimes we don't. To this day, I can't control my son's energy levels, but I can control the amount of toys in our home and the number of activities on the calendar.

My biggest saboteur as a new mom was busyness. I wasn't really competing with my son in a battle for energy. I felt so tired because I gave too much of my time to the rest of the world—time needed for mothering and homemaking.

Saboteurs are the obstacles that work against us in performing our duties as home managers. These are the distractions and situations that render us ineffective in all of our roles—not just the ones relating to keeping a clean house. Sometimes we call them excuses.

Let's look at some of the saboteurs that prevent us from keeping presentable homes:

BUSYNESS

My calendar was inundated with activities. I always had things to do, places to go, and friends to meet. People wondered about me, *Is she having an affair with her Daytimer?*

I didn't leave enough open time to focus on cleaning. On those occasions when I had the time, I used those extra precious hours to recuperate from my busy schedule. I finally decided to create some margin where we don't make commitments. Maintain free space in your calendar so the busyness of life won't trip you up in your housekeeping efforts.

You've probably heard the phrase, "Idle hands are the devil's workshop." There's also an acronym for BUSY that says, "Being Under Satan's Yoke." Margin is God's gift to us. We seek balance in our lives, but we will find it in the margins.

TIME WASTERS

Playing on the computer, yakking on the phone, and opening junk mail are prime examples of time wasters. How many times have you opened a computer game to play for just a few minutes only to find yourself still playing hours later? I admit, I'm guilty. How often do you talk on the phone when you know you should be doing something else? I can't begin to count how many times I call my sister because I don't feel like cleaning. Sometimes junk mail disguises itself as an official looking letter. Don't we all end up opening that at some point?

Other timewasters include watching television, excessive napping, leisure shopping, and watching the wind blow by. Anything so we don't have to clean.

POOR HEALTH

Sometimes our homes suffer because of specific physical or mental ailments. Even something that seems as innocuous as the common cold can throw a wrench in our cleaning abilities. For individuals with chronic ailments, the best thing to do is see your doctors regularly and follow his or her advice.

When taking medicines with extreme side effects, others may have to help with the workload. If finances allow, hire someone to help you instead of expecting to do it yourself with a broken leg. The housework will always be there. Take care of yourself first.

Diagnoses such as clinical depression can interfere with the desire for a clean home. When I'm feeling down from a these-pants-make-me-look-fat day or a bad hair day, I'm not motivated to clean. I can't imagine what it must be like for someone who struggles with depression. If you think you suffer from depression, see a doctor immediately. Find a counselor willing to collaborate with a professional organizer. Accept whatever help you need to get your house and life back in order.

EXHAUSTION

When we're too tired to clean, what can we do? If it was only as simple as taking an extra nap! But it's not that easy.

A pediatrician friend told me that when a baby has a fever, the fever is only a symptom of the attacking virus. But we still treat the fever. Likewise, while exhaustion is just a symptom of something else, we treat the fatigue.

So how do we treat exhaustion? Allocate time for extra bed rest. Treat yourself to a massage. Drop some activities from your schedule. Slow down. Participate in a retreat. Eat healthier. Drink more water.

Determine the root cause of the fatigue. Is it due to schedule overload or something else? Busyness, stress, and poor health all contribute to feeling tired. Visit your doctor to rule out medical causes.

There was a time when I experienced extreme fatigue. It was a major battle to get out of bed and brush my teeth. Physically unable to do much, the house was a disaster. I checked with my doctor so he could cure what I thought to be Chronic Fatigue Syndrome. It turns out that total and utter exhaustion is a symptom of pregnancy.

BARGAIN HUNTING

My husband says there are two seasons: church season and flea market season. During flea market season, he's quicker than a speeding bullet to get in and out of our house of worship so he can hunt for bargains. Like a hunter circling his prey, he persuades the vendors into practically giving things away. And he actually has been known to bring home dead animals—at least the taxidermied heads of them. He impressed me beyond measure with his ability to find good things at cheap prices. After we stuffed our garage with all these amazing deals, we started realizing that maybe we don't need to buy something just because the price is right. Our eagerness to buy lots of inexpensive stuff sabotaged our goal of space in the garage for our cars.

Who can resist a good sale? If you lack that kind of discipline, avoid garage sales, flea markets, and auctions. Remember, one person's trash is not always another person's treasure.

FREEBIES

Free stuff is fun. But it's not always good, especially when we're trying to de-clutter.

My sister accumulated an overload of toys and clothes for her girls because people passed on their old stuff to her. She accepted anything people offered. When her friends got rid of stuff, they always knew they could dump it off at her house. It's okay to accept donations, but only if they're needed. It's so tempting to take something just because it's free.

Fairgrounds, festivals, and expos are notorious for their junk giveaways. Freebie novelty items abound. They give new meaning to the word *clean sweep* for clutterbugs. My mother loved going to the county fair because of all the freebies she could bring home. Her version of a clean sweep was not cleaning the house but clearing the freebie tables at the fair of all their goodies. If a booth was giving away pencils, she and her beach-bag-sized purse breezed along the side of the table as she casually swept them into her bag. Do you do that too? Not in the same league as my mother, I never performed a clean sweep such as that, but I am guilty of taking a few extra now and then.

BAD HELPER BOUNDARIES

Most of us like to help others when we can. But sometimes we have to help ourselves before taking on the Good Samaritan role. Airplane safety procedures require passengers holding a baby to put the oxygen masks on themselves first. After the parent or guardian is getting oxygen, then they can take care of the little one.

How does this relate to de-cluttering? It goes back to not storing other people's stuff. But it also goes beyond that into the realm of saving clutter we think will help other people.

While visiting my sister's home a few years back, I noticed two large trash bags full of toys slumped on her kitchen floor. She explained the toys were for a friend. When confronted on how long these bags sat waiting to be picked up, she acknowledged them sitting there for "just a couple months." Just a couple months? That's more than eight weeks of junk cluttering up her kitchen! Fortunately, her big sister—me—was there to set her straight.

When saving items to give away, tell the intended recipient to pick it up a by a certain date. If that bag of stuff is still sitting there after the deadline, then donate it or throw it out.

PROCRASTINATION

For now and *later* should be banned from our vocabularies. They are bad words, yet I humbly confess that sometimes I still use them.

"I'll just put that item here *for now*."

"Oh, I'll clean that up *later*."

Create permanent homes for things. Then you don't have to find temporary dwellings. A *for now* attitude means more work later. Things stashed in places they don't belong add clutter to those areas. When we forget where we put things *for now*, we spend extra time later looking for lost items or end up purchasing duplicates.

Get into the habit of cleaning as you go. When you complete an activity, think "Clean *now*!" instead of "I'll get to it *later*." Put away your belongings as soon as you're through with them and wipe up any mess. To avoid more work later, throw out trash immediately.

Just as compounding interest on a credit card leads to out-of-control debt, compounding interest on trash leads to out-of-control housework. Consider:

- We eat dinner. Food falls on the floor. We step on the food. Our footsteps create a path of crumbs. We set an important paper on the floor. It becomes encrusted with grease and crumbs.

- Newspapers are left all over the floor. They rip when people walk on them. The cat tries to eat the paper and tears it to shreds. The baby plays with the shredded paper and drags it all over the house.
- Mail gets tossed on the kitchen table. To clear the table for dinner, we stick it in the nearest drawer. We keep repeating this habit. The drawer becomes full. Then we have to sort through an entire drawer mixed with personal correspondence, bills, and junk mail.

GIFTS

Gifts are probably the biggest saboteurs by sheer physical volume. Presents of all kinds crowded my house and cluttered my life. My obese home suffered from a lot of gift fat on both the giving and receiving ends. Gift clutter sprawled in every room. My family, friends, and I were generous to a fault—overgenerous.

We don't need to be everyone's personal Santa. It's okay not to give a sack full of presents to everyone you know for birthdays and holidays. Sometimes less is more. I've learned that when I give less, people appreciate what I give more.

For my husband's birthday one year I bought him a wheelbarrow and as many gifts as I could fit inside it. He sped from one present to the next, ferociously tearing off the wrapping paper, and barely pausing to see what I got for him. Now, I try to be creative and not overwhelm him with so much stuff. It makes the experience more special. He never lets me forget the Christmas I bought him a few small stocking stuffers and a wallet. Inside that wallet, I gave him money to buy what he wanted instead of a bunch of junk to clutter our home.

On the receiving end, I now find more joy in receiving fewer gifts. What's important is that I'm remembered, even if it's with a phone call or greeting card. For my birthday, I tell my husband that the best gift he can give me is cooking and cleaning for the day so I don't have to do anything. We may eat pizza on paper plates for breakfast, lunch, and dinner, but I'm happy because I get a time-out from my kitchen duties.

Simplifying our giving is a key to defeating the saboteur that presents itself in beautiful wrapping paper and big, shiny bows. Let others know before holidays that you'd like to forego a gift exchange—or at least minimize it. Cap the number of gifts or limit the amount of money for each party to spend. If space is an issue, ask givers to keep the size of gifts within certain dimension. A friend of mine told her overgenerous parents that if the gift didn't fit in a shirt box, then it was too big for her house.

Before deciding on a gift to buy, don't just ask if the recipient would like it. Ask yourself if this gift will enhance his or her life or just add clutter.

Search for creative gift ideas. When my nieces were young, I gave them panties for birthdays and Christmas. Plain underwear doesn't make an impression, so I went the extra mile and paid a few dollars more for something I knew they would like—such as panties with their favorite cartoon characters etched on them. I figured this made a good gift because it wasn't clutter. Growing kids need new underwear.

You don't need to spend tons of money on young children. I could give my son a bunch of empty boxes and he'd build a fort or a robot with them. When he's done with them, there's no buyer's remorse when these boxes end up in the trash or recycle bin.

Ask friends and family what they need—not what they want. Most people confuse wants with needs anyway, but at least this way you have a better chance of giving something that won't clutter their homes.

One year, my sister asked for bathroom tissue for Christmas. She said that she was always running out of it and having extra around wouldn't clutter her home. Her husband responded by purchasing one of those giant boxes filled with 40 rolls of bathroom tissue sold at warehouse clubs. She loved it because it met a need at a time of year—Christmas—when her house gets besieged by clutter. However, make sure your loved one asks for something like this first. Getting a new trash pail for your birthday doesn't say "I love you" unless you ask for it.

What kinds of gifts make great presents and prevent clutter? Whether giving or receiving, consider the following ideas:

- Family picture, framed
- Time together, perhaps a treat to dinner
- Babysitting
- Entertainment tickets to a movie or play
- Entertainment Book (a special coupon book sold across the country, usually associated with fundraising)
- Food club membership
- Gas card
- Gift certificate to a restaurant, coffeehouse, or grocery store
- Gift card to a favorite department store
- Baked goods
- Certificate for a massage or a trip to the hair salon
- Cash

SPECIAL SITUATIONS

Sometimes life just happens and we have to deal with it. Your spouse gets deployed overseas for months on end or travels a lot for his civilian job. Your child gets sick. Another child gets diagnosed with a learning disability. You sprain your ankle. When things like this happen, don't play the role of a martyr. Reach out to others for help.

New circumstances present challenges all the time—sometimes by choice. This means revisiting our decisions and adapting to their consequences. Here are some examples:

You decide to go back to school. It's more work than you thought. The following semester, you take one graduate level course instead of three. On the other hand, you could decide this isn't the right season of life to go back to college.

You accept a promotion at work that requires working longer hours. You're not making more money once you add the extra time you put into your job, so you step down from your promotion. Or you could choose to continue in your current position while applying for a better job elsewhere.

You sign up as a work-from-home independent sales distributor selling jewelry or makeup—and now store inventory at home. You discover there is extra work involved with housing all of those products that clutter your home. So you decide to carry a smaller amount of inventory, choosing the minimum you need in order to sell your product at home shows. Then again, you might decide to get out of the business altogether as you discover the amount of paperwork involved doesn't fit into your vision of simplifying your life.

You adopt a pet from the humane society. You thought you could keep up with the extra work, but it's proving to be too much. You don't want to give up your pet, so you purchase a doggie gate to contain the shedding to one room. Or maybe you realize you already own three dogs and three is enough; so you contact an animal rescue organization to help you find a new home for your newly adopted dog.

WHEN SABOTEURS STRIKE

Here's a quick defense for those times you feel sabotaged in your battle against clutter. When you're feeling too busy, too tired, too ill, or otherwise lack motivation, at a minimum do these three things:

1. Put the dishes in the dishwasher and run it.
2. Start and complete one load of laundry.
3. Set your timer for eight minutes. Use that time for whatever other cleaning and de-cluttering you can get done—not including loading your dishwasher and washing machine.

Become familiar with the saboteurs of a clean home before they cause problems. Do the best you can with the time, energy, and resources you have. Then, as the potential saboteurs create obstacles to maintaining a presentable home, make the necessary changes to overcome them.

SOMETHING TO THINK ABOUT

- What seem like saboteurs, but really aren't? What are the real saboteurs?
- What are the biggest saboteurs—or excuses—in your life that prevent you from creating the kind of home you desire?
- What changes can you make to defeat the obstacles that work against a clean home?
- How do you feel about the way your family exchanges gifts? What suggestions can you make to maintain the valued traditions of celebrations while reducing the potential clutter?
- What special situations are you facing that present new challenges to keeping a presentable home? What are your options to overcome those challenges?

HOMEBUILDING

Above all else, guard your heart, for it is the wellspring of life. —*Proverbs 4:23*

We guard our homes from thieves and people with ill intentions. Are we doing the same for our hearts? What saboteurs do you fall victim to—money, power, possessions, entertainment, work, unhealthy relationships? Don't give your heart to something that can't love you back—or to someone who won't love you back. Seek out safe relationships where you can be yourself. Start by offering your heart to God. Let Him be the source of your wellspring.

11 MONEY TALKS, CLUTTER WALKS

ONE of the biggest excuses I've seen for accumulating clutter is saving money. We buy something because it's a bargain, not because we need it. We reason that we might be able to use it someday. And if we can't use it, we can give it as a gift, right?

You just can't beat those sale prices. We think bargains save us money, but fail to realize that every dollar spent is one less dollar saved. While the sales circulars may read, "Buy 2 and save $20," we must to say to ourselves, "Buy zero and save the entire cost of the purchase!"

Whether it's an expensive ornament, a cheap trinket, or a sale item, it's worth nothing if we don't need it and it adds clutter to our lives. It's not a good deal if we won't use it. When we purchase too much stuff, the resulting clutter costs more than the few pennies saved.

But what if I can't get the same item later at its current low price?

I have news for you. There will always be another sale.

I'm not saying don't buy sale items. My point is, don't buy something just because it's on sale when you don't really need it. As you de-clutter, ask these questions when you go shopping:

Do I really need it?

Do I really love it?

Can I afford it without having to put it on a credit card?

How expensive is it to maintain?

Is it easy to clean?

Regardless of cost, is this a quality item?

How often will I use it?

SEVEN MONEY-SAVING TIPS
TO REDUCE CLUTTER

1. Cancel and pay off credit cards.

How many credit cards are nestled inside your wallet? Accompanying each card you hold comes a monthly bill, yearly statements, and insurance offers. Tired of the hassle of so much extra paperwork, I got rid of my credit cards. While most people like to keep one in case of an emergency, I cancelled them all. I can already hear those "But what ifs" coming.

- *"But what if I'm faced with an emergency?"* The Bible tells us to expect problems. Jesus says, "In this world you will have trouble." Not we *might* have trouble, but we *will* have trouble. Yet, aren't we surprised when our car breaks down or when we are confronted with an unexpected illness or when Christmas comes? Not planning for the unexpected, we turn to our credit cards. Since I know there will be emergencies, I plan for them by setting aside an emergency fund. What that doesn't cover, I trust God to handle.

- *"But what if I need to make hotel or airline reservations—don't I need a credit card for that?"* With the advent of debit cards, we no longer need credit cards for reserving a room or a flight. Most banks now offer debit card holders the same protection as credit card holders.

- *"But what if a business won't take payment by debit cards?"* If a place does not accept a debit card, then my business goes elsewhere. Simple as that.

You may disagree about eliminating all of your credit cards, but I challenge you to consider keeping only one. De-clutter your wallet. Start setting aside money so you so don't have to rely on plastic.

2. Live in a cash only society.

What does living by cash only look like? Pay cash instead of burning your credit card when you grab a coffee at your favorite coffeehouse.

Use cash rather than a debit card to buy groceries. Hand the cashier cash from your wallet rather than a check when purchasing clothes.

Just because the rest of the world pays for things by check or plastic doesn't mean you have to follow suit. Psychologically, it hurts more to spend cash than it does to write a check or use debit or credit. If we pay by cash, we buy less stuff.

3. Establish a budget.

Allocating a certain amount of money for weekly expenses prevents us from spending money on things we don't really need. If I'm left with no entertainment money after going out for dinner and a movie, I skip my latte at the coffee shop. I won't buy those party supplies if there's not enough in my grocery budget when I already have plain paper plates at home.

The most effective method I found for staying within my budget is the envelope system. You don't need to buy anything fancy, regular envelopes will do. Mark one for groceries, one for gas money, one for entertainment money, and so forth. If you have kids, create spending envelopes for them too. Not only will it prevent you from buying unnecessary toy clutter, but it teaches valuable lessons to your kids. Let them learn that if you allocate ten dollars for *you* to spend on them each week outside of their allowance, then that money will only go so far.

Speaking of allowances, I'm not a big believer in them. I refuse to pay my son for making his bed. As an adult, no one pays me for making my bed. This is called reality parenting.

And the reality is we all need to live within our budgets. When we do, it helps prevent clutter from invading our homes, hearts, and minds.

4. Practice "just in time" buying.

This has made the biggest difference in my battle against clutter. I used to buy stuff for future use whenever it was on sale. Not anymore.

I once thought buying items in advance of when I needed them would save me lots of money. I was known for buying Christmas and birthday gifts several months ahead of time as I discovered great bargains on gift items throughout the year. Then one day I realized I was not saving money, and those presents cluttered up my home.

- I misplaced gifts and ended up buying replacement presents.
- I simply found more stuff to buy and gave more.
- I changed my mind about gifts, bought something else, but kept the original gifts.
- I had to buy different gifts because the recipients no longer wanted or needed the items because I bought their presents too early.

If you buy gift items too far in advance, returns could be an issue. You learn your nephew outgrows his superhero phase by the time his birthday comes around, but the store may not accept the return or offer an exchange. All those cool action figures you bought him now belong to you. So they continue to clutter your home.

Do you really want to add the extra work of tracking all the gift receipts from items you bought months in advance? Will the stores even provide refunds if the items need to be returned a year after the purchase date? If you have issues with clutter, is it a wise decision to store gifts months ahead of time?

Consider how much it costs you to buy birthday gifts six months ahead of time. Do you lose them and end up buying something else? Do you end up wasting money because for whatever reason you give something else—or more—than the original gift item?

Evaluate how much it costs you to buy Christmas gifts in July. Do you find more stuff to give and end up over-gifting? And what about greeting cards—even though you bought holiday cards in January at seventy-five percent off, are you buying new ones again in November?

You don't have to wait until Christmas Eve to do all of your holiday shopping, but you don't need to start on December 26 for next year either. Be smart about it.

This is what just-in-time buying looks like for me these days regarding gift items:

- I refrain from purchasing presents for people more than three months in advance of their birthday or Christmas. As my son gets older, I track the months his friends celebrate birthdays in order to plan for them.

- I write down what I buy and for whom—especially for Christmas gifts—to prevent over-gifting. I also try to note special interests in order to be more thoughtful when purchasing presents. I jot down gift ideas as I think of them so I can be on the lookout for the items to go on sale.

- I allocate shopping time on my schedule for known celebrations. Christmas comes every year, so it's not a surprise. My son's birthday comes at the same time every year, so it's not an unexpected event. When I'm not in a rush, I make more thoughtful decisions on the gift I buy. Likewise, I don't start too soon just to get the shopping over. I choose to be intentional.

- I look for gifts that won't take a lot of storage space in my home if I need to hold on to them for more than a week. As much as I would like to stop buying gifts altogether, they are part of our cultural norms. I can't give a gift card to everyone for every occasion. So I think about how much space something will take up in my home until I give it to the recipient.

- I don't let the time management issues of others become my problem. If my son receives a last minute invitation to a birthday party, I don't run to the store without a second to spare. My son has received invites as late as the day before the party. We either decline the invitation, or accept and allow the birthday boy or girl to wait a few extra days for their gift from us. Sure, I could load up a closet or bin with items for occasions such as that, but I don't want to. I live in a small house where my indoor real estate comes at a premium.

But when it came to purchasing items for future use, I didn't stop at gift items. There's more. And all this stuff cost money and required storage space in my home. I used to stock my pantry so full that you'd think we weren't going to be near a grocery store for a year. When I was pregnant, I started collecting home-schooling materials up to the fifth grade level. Family members helped me pack my baby's closet so full that he had clothes that would fit going into kindergarten.

And let me tell you about my books. It was my dream to own a personal library. Hundreds—and I do mean hundreds—of books piled in bookshelves, in closets, boxes, and on the floors waited patiently for me to rescue them. I bought them, planning to read each one someday. But there were just too many books and not enough time to sort through them to find the one particular book on my latest topic of interest. So I bought the same one again.

Here's what just-in-time buying looks like in other areas of my life:

• As my son grows up, I only buy clothes in his size or the next size up. No size 14 will sit in storage for a couple years if he wears a size 8.

• I refrain from purchasing high school homeschool curriculum when my son is still in early elementary school. I also meet him where he is. If he's advanced in science, but struggles in reading, then I don't let the grade level on the curriculum dictate what I use.

• I buy new kitchen appliances only when I need them. I might need a new steamer someday, but not today. So, I will save that money rather than spending it on something I will not use right away.

• I plan meals by the week and don't go overboard in grocery shopping. Sure, I keep a few extra non-perishable staples on hand, but I don't buy so many canned and boxed goods that I have to give them homes outside the kitchen.

• Instead of buying every book I *might* like to read someday, I buy only those that I'm ready to begin reading in the next couple weeks. I ask myself if I have the time to read it in the near future and what titles on my bookshelf am I willing to part with to make room for a new book. For every new book I bring home, I try to find two to get rid of. I don't need a home library anymore—we have a great public library in our community. I can get just about anything I need there.

How about you? What do you collect? What do you have stashed around the house to use someday? How long are you saving those party supplies to use someday? Are you buying duplicate scrapbook supplies because you can't find the ones you purchased eight months ago? Do you buy new clothes for your kids so far in advance that when they fit they are no longer in style?

There's a freedom in buying what you need when you need it. Nothing gets lost or damaged. You don't have to stress about losing the receipt if you need to return something. There's no reason to worry if the store will accept the return. You're not buying extra because you found the same item in a different style you like better. Duplicates and triplicates of things aren't invading your home because you can't locate the original. You don't have to worry about your brother buying himself a fishing rod just like the one you bought to give him next Christmas.

Not only does "just-in-time buying" save you extra money, it saves you from extra clutter!

5. Stop cutting coupons.

Stop cutting coupons to save money—can that be right? It sure is! Coupons are mini-advertisements to market products we would not normally buy. Some people with loads of discipline can save money with coupons. People who struggle with clutter tend not to fall in this category. We cut coupons and forget about them. When we use them, we often purchase things that would not have made it on our grocery list without the coupon. They are enticements to buy more stuff. And when we don't use them, the coupons clutter our homes.

If you struggle with keeping a presentable home and find coupons cluttering your house, give the couponing a rest—at least until you get a hold on the clutter.

6. Create a coin jar.

Loose change. Yes, even coins are clutter when they're scattered about the house. Use a piggy bank, mason jar, or other container as a home for spare change. Do not include this money in your monthly budget. Save it until the jar is full. Then treat yourself to something special. Preferably something that won't clutter your home, like a massage or a new hairstyle.

My son likes to fill a pencil bag with coins he finds around the house. He goes on coin hunts underneath the couch cushions, on the floorboards in the car, and in the laundry room. He calls this bag of coins his emergency money. When a trip to the ice cream parlor is not in the budget on a hot summer day, he'll pull out his emergency money and treat both of us. Not only does he help keep the house clear of coin clutter that fell out of pockets, he also learns the value of money.

7. Stop borrowing money and buying things on credit.

Financing plans, car loans, student loans, personal loans—any type of borrowing—clutter our homes with more stuff, our mailboxes with more bills, our schedules with more headaches, and our relationships with more stress.

Why do we buy new automobiles that lose thirty to forty percent of their value as soon as we drive them off the lot and then pay interest on them for another four or five years? While used automobiles provide better value, if we have to borrow money, then maybe we need to consider the fact that we just can't afford it. Think about the emotional clutter from that big car payment every month.

Also, we don't have to buy things simply because we can afford the monthly payment. We might be able to afford the payment now, but we don't know what the future holds. If you're making monthly payments on the new in-ground pool you had installed, but can't afford groceries because you lost your job, that stresses you out. It adds clutter to your mind and heart.

Experience the freedom that comes from delayed gratification. My husband, yearning for a big, European, military truck called a Unimog, urged me to borrow money with him so he could buy one. I told him that if he wanted a Unimog, we needed to save up the money. So we did, and then we had a big, old, ugly Unimog cluttering our driveway. He didn't use this gas-guzzling vehicle much, but he liked to look at it and admired it until he sold it. The best part was that every time he looked at it, he was looking at a vehicle that was paid for. It was a good feeling.

Let's talk student loans. I made the mistake of borrowing a lot of money through student loans, and decades later I'm still paying for that mistake. I viewed it as an investment in me. The only problem is that I can't sell my college degree to help pay off the loan as people do if they get over their heads in house or car payments. Education is not an appreciable asset. I mortgaged my future based on the hope my college education would pay off.

Deciding that the profession of motherhood is far greater than any career, I chose to be a stay-at-home mom. I don't get paid for being my kid's mom, but I still have to pay that student loan. Now that my son has been diagnosed with autism, those monthly payments could be used toward special therapies not covered by insurance. Since then, I've met many friends who entered a career field completely different from what they studied or dropped out of school altogether. And those working in their degree field often find it doesn't pay enough to make those monthly student loan payments. That's a lot of financial clutter in our mailboxes and on our minds.

Moving on to personal loans—they are the worst. My husband and I borrowed $2000 from my in-laws to use toward our first house. It created tension between us—and that was certainly not their fault. It was just that I didn't like owing money to them. I felt indebted to my in-laws. That added some relational clutter I didn't need.

So what about mortgages? Is that debt okay? It's more accurate to call it tolerable. Since we either have to pay rent or mortgage, at least with a mortgage, the payments eventually end. But we can shoot for smaller monthly payments in a smaller house. Less square footage equals lower heating costs. Less money is spent on decorating and landscaping. A smaller house means less area to clean. Above all, smaller homes hold less clutter.

And let's not forget cosigning on someone else's loan. That's almost the same as taking out a loan yourself. Instead of you making the payment every month, you worry if your loved one remembers to make the payment. If they falter, their debt becomes your debt. You are doing no favors by helping a family member build a credit score by cosigning a loan. Let them build their credit scores by paying rent and utilities on time.

If you feel defeated by debt, consider enrolling in Dave Ramsey's *Financial Peace University*. He will give you the special training you need to fight your money battles and break free from the clutter caused by debt. You can learn more about this program at daveramsey.com.

DEBT AND CLUTTER

Let's dig deeper in the relationship between debt and clutter. It takes money to buy the things that end up littering our homes. We charge more stuff on our credit cards that become clutter. Then we keep paying for our junk because it costs money to maintain it, insure it, clean it, and store it. Our pocketbooks get thinner and our homes grow fatter.

And then there's the incidental clutter associated with debt. Each monthly bill brings more papers to track. Credit card receipts cram our wallets. Billing statements end up scattered throughout our homes, some with payment checks inside them. We open new store accounts to save that extra ten percent, but pay more in finance charges and late fees down the road.

Debt clogs our minds. We stress over the money we owe. We think about our payment deadline and if we'll have enough money to cover the minimum monthly payment.

Debt steals our time. We waste hours shopping sales to charge stuff on credit. Then we spend more time writing out checks for each credit card bill. More check writing means more time for balancing our checkbooks. Sometimes we misplace our bills and lose hours of time as we frantically search for our statements. Then, when we don't pay promptly, we lose chunks of our days responding to collectors.

Debt eats away at our relationships. Relationships deteriorate from arguing over our spending habits, including the stuff we bought and the things we want to buy. We even find ourselves fighting over the clutter in our homes caused by warehousing items we are still paying for. We don't enjoy living surrounded by clutter. But we love our possessions too much to give them away, throw them away, or sell them. So our debts increase as we finance all of our heart's desires, and our relationships pay the toll.

Debt. It clutters our homes, minds, schedules, and relationships. If you have debt, get rid of it. If you are free of it, stay away from it.

SOMETHING TO THINK ABOUT

- A. Divide the home's square footage by the monthly payment Square footage = Cost per square foot rent or mortgage.
  B. Multiply the cost per square foot by the number of square feet allocated for storage. (Cost per square foot) x (total square feet of storage room) = Cost of storage space.
- In what areas can you reduce spending to cut down the flow of clutter?
- What kinds of invisible clutter does debt cause in your life?
- How will you incorporate the concept of just-in-time buying into your shopping habits?
- How do you plan to pay off debt? What habits do you need to change to become a better money manager?

HOMEBUILDING

Keep your lives free from the love of money and be content with what you have, because God has said, "Never will I leave you; never will I forsake you." —Hebrews 13:5

How eager are you to attain more and more stuff? Are your pocketbooks pierced with a grief called debt? Or have you embraced a lifestyle of contentment?

Start praying for contentment. Trust in the Lord to fulfill your needs. Stop depending on plastic and start relying on God.

12 BREAKING FREE

"I hear you live in a messy house!" my childhood playmate accused. "Is that true?" Her eyes squinted in anger. Her condemning voice rang through my ears.

"No," I lied, "that's not true."

While other neighborhood children invited playmates inside their homes, no friends were allowed inside my house. And after that confrontation, I feared what anyone would say who stepped through our front door.

TOO MUCH STUFF

By the time I reached elementary school, I mastered the art of *mess* and fully embraced the *too much stuff* lifestyle. To say I kept a messy bedroom would be an understatement. But I also commandeered the "quick clean" technique. If threatened with losing playtime, I simply kicked all the stuff on my floor under the bed.

I never felt I had enough stuff, always wanting more. Though I lived in abundance, it felt as if I had so little. There were too many toys to play with, but not much of value. I owned lots of clothes, but only a few nice outfits. Plenty of electronics, jewelry, stationery, books, and games cluttered my room, but what did I have to show for it? Lack of organizational skills. Lost and broken items. No discipline.

As I grew older, toys, papers, clothes, and other collections increased. Likewise, the available space between my floor and box spring decreased, forcing me to find a new place to put all my things.

☐ ☐ ☐

"You will stay inside this house all weekend unless you clean your room!" my mother scolded.

"No problem!" I slyly replied. This ten-year old had a plan.

A couple of hours later, I informed my mother that I had finished cleaning my room.

"I need to inspect it first," she responded in disbelief. After all, how could I have cleaned such a big mess in so short a time?

Mother slowly made her way upstairs to my bedroom. Her eyes nearly popped out of their sockets. Astonished with my thorough cleaning job, she stared at the clear floor, my neatly made bed, and clutter-free dresser tops.

"Wow! It looks good!" she said as her eyes scanned the room. Then she paused for a moment and glanced back at the bed.

"You shoved everything under the bed, didn't you?" Expecting to catch me cheating, she stooped to her knees and checked. "Well, where did you put everything?"

"It's put away," I replied.

Mother walked toward the closet door.

Uh oh, I thought, *I hope she doesn't check inside there.*

As Mother turned the handle, I held my breath, preparing for her reaction. Clothes, toys, electronics, along with other odds and ends tumbled out of my stuffed closet. Jam packed from floor to ceiling, this avalanche of things cascaded down, spoiling my clear floor.

Red faced, my mother yelled, "You will clean this up *now!* And you're grounded!"

I shoved many of the fallen items under the bed, stuffed what was left back in the closet, and pulled out my extra large, adult travel suitcase holding over fifty Barbies and all their accessories. *Playtime!*

☐ ☐ ☐

Living in a messy home has the potential to cause physical harm too.

My school drama club cast me in the role of Violet in *Charlie and the Chocolate Factory*. I wanted to be Veruca, the bad egg. I related to her. She wanted everything and she wanted it all now.

One day after play practice, a bee buzzed around my head. I dashed inside the house with the bee in hot pursuit. The buzz sounded as if it were circling me once inside the doorway. I felt like a helpless swimmer surrounded by sharks. I ran to the living room and tripped over a book as I fled for safety.

My ankle swelled to the size of a baseball. A visit to the doctor revealed I separated a growth plate. Required to wear a cast, I limped on crutches for six weeks, and my acting career ended. Just like that.

I looked for someone to blame, but the book on the floor was part of the encyclopedia set I used earlier in the week to write a report for class.

CLEANING REFLECTIONS

As a child, my cleaning contributions were minimal, but my clutter donations remained quite generous. I rarely threw things out, often received lots of stuff, and consistently overvalued possessions. And all the time, I believed that none of the mess was my fault.

When my mother instructed me to pick up my toys, I refused unless coerced with threats. When she told me to clean my room, I snapped back, "Only if you clean yours first!" I certainly avoided any chores she attempted to delegate to me. After all, why should I be required to clean when my mother didn't pick up the house to my expectations? She should be the one setting the example, right?

I was a spoiled, rotten brat, but I did have a heart. There were times when I tried to help, even wanted to help, but more often I found better things to do than clean. Like staring at the leaves falling off the trees outside, watching the dog sleep, or doing homework. In fact, a root canal sounded more fun than picking up all the stuff lying around the house.

And then there was dinner time. Dining at home proved to be a disaster we all wanted to avoid. Dishes were often piled high in the kitchen sink, and nobody wanted to tackle that job. Eating out was the rule, not the exception.

Did I ever offer to wash the dishes? Nope, not that I can remember. Besides, that was Mom's job. Why would I want to volunteer for it? Until the dishes were clean again, I didn't mind using paper plates and plastic utensils.

I didn't view housekeeping as my responsibility, but I did help dirty the dishes; I added to the laundry and left toys on the floor. My shoes brought dust, leaves, pebbles, mud, and slush in from the yard. I left fingerprints on the counters and door handles. But no, I did not help clean the house. I placed all of the blame on my mother. Not realizing I was responsible for *some* of the mess, I let my mother take responsibility for *all* of the mess.

When I was fifteen years old, I finally decided to clean the living room while my mother went shopping. I wanted to start there because everybody used that room, and it was the messiest place in our home.

Newspapers and magazines cluttered the outskirts of the living room floor. A layer of dog hair was plastered to the carpet. Mounds of laundry waited on the couches to be folded. Scattered toys lay forgotten in every corner. Every shelf and table bore the weight of too much stuff.

I bagged up expired coupons, old newspapers, food wrappers, and other trash. Anything my mother needed to sort through, I put in boxes.

Upon her return home, my mother expressed her displeasure at me for messing up *her* room. "What have you done? Why did you touch my things?" Spying the expired coupons in the trash bags, she screamed, "Why did you throw them all out? There could be one I can still use!"

She dumped the bags filled with trash right in the middle of the clean floor. Any flicker of desire to help with housework was buried under that mess.

Later I realized my mother's attachment to stuff, including the garbage, went beyond what I misjudged as laziness. Her issues went beyond the understanding of a teenager. All I felt then was that the trash was more important to her than I was.

Yearning for peace and a sense of order, the disarray engulfed me like a tornado. Home never became a haven to run to—it was a whirlwind of mess and clutter to run away from.

To be sure, I experienced happy times with my family. But piles and boxes and bags of clutter overshadow many of the joyful memories.

MAKING PEACE

Looking back, I recognize that my mother's problem of too much stuff was symptomatic of far deeper issues.

My mother didn't want to live in a messy house. She expressed desire for something better. I remember watching her do laundry or wash dishes, but the work seemed to pile up faster than she could keep up with it. And more stuff flowing into the house put her even further behind. Hours of catch-up cleaning only proved how much more needed to be done. In my mother's world, the cleaning was never finished.

As an adult, I developed a good relationship with my mother—despite the cluttered home in which I grew up. In the end, she did help me learn to keep a clean house. She taught me by example that:

- Dishes left to a "fairy godwasher" linger dirty in the sink.
- Shelves covered with armies of knickknacks are difficult to dust.
- Holding on to unneeded clothes creates mountains of laundry.

I don't blame my mother for what she didn't teach me, but I am grateful for what I learned.

A NEW DAY

My growing-up years taught me some hard lessons. I lived in a messy house and kept a messy bedroom; I thought cleaning would come naturally once I moved out on my own. But I continued to find excuse after excuse for not cleaning:

"I don't have the time. I'm just too busy."

"My husband (or job or schoolwork) is too demanding."

"If I had more storage bins, I could get this place clean."

Excuses aside, the real reason was that the clutter was always in the way. I had too much stuff.

Finally, I asked myself, "Am I willing to give up the clutter for a clean house?" I loved my stuff, but not enough to continue sacrificing my quality of life. In return for a presentable home, I gave up the clutter.

Surprisingly, de-cluttering didn't feel like hard work because once I got started, I experienced how fun it was to let go of things. It took me a year of consistent de-cluttering until my home reached a manageable point. Here's what that looks like:

- Flat surfaces generally remain clear of clutter. Important documents no longer get lost in a sea of stuff.
- People don't walk in my home and wonder if I just moved in because of boxes stacked against walls in every room.
- Closets hold items in a reasonably organized fashion. Frustration levels decreased, because I don't have to go on a scavenger hunt to locate the valuables stashed on crowded shelves piled with junk.
- The food in my pantry gets used. No more buying duplicates of things I can't find.
- My bedroom is not overrun by laundry. The clothes in my dresser actually fit and look good on me.

And people see me differently from my too-much-stuff days. They tell me I'm more relationship focused. Instead of spending so much time shopping and tending to all my stuff, friends notice me making time for them. Plus, my communication skills have improved without all the distractions from images of too much stuff lurking in the back of my mind. I don't experience brain fog from thinking about all the clutter.

Gone are the days of clinging to every so-called sacred treasure—junk that wasn't even garage sale caliber. No more shoving things under my bed and cramming stuff in closets. Throwing the clutter out brings me joy and a sense of liberation.

Today, homemaking is an expression of love, not a dreaded task. I once avoided dirty dishes like the plague they might have carried. Now, I enjoy the sight of clean and neatly stacked plates in my cupboard. Sure, there are days I still struggle to stay on top of things, but I'm no longer overwhelmed by the thought of cleaning. I feel confident in my ability to create a nice home for my family.

As I look back at how far I've come, I still have areas that need improvement. New challenges present themselves on a daily basis. My son takes out all of the blankets from the linen closet and makes a fort in my bedroom closet. There goes my neatly organized wardrobe. The washing machine breaks causing me to fall behind on laundry. I return from vacation too tired to unpack my bags, so they lay in the middle of the floor while I recover from my holiday travels. There's always something. However, these minor setbacks do not sentence me to defeat. The war has already been won.

So how did I break free from the chains of possession overload? Was it years of therapy? A magic medication? A reality television home makeover? No. My desire for stuff dwindled after I learned to trust in God in areas I didn't know faith issues existed.

A slave to my collections of junk, my possessions owned me. I never realized I was in bondage to clutter. On my own, there's no way I could have let go of my passion for too much stuff. When I asked God to reclaim the area in my heart consumed by the pursuit for material things, I began to trust in Him instead of trusting in stuff:

- I don't have to stockpile a year's worth of food. If I'm ever caught with an empty pantry in a natural or man-made disaster, I know my family will be just fine. God will provide.
- It won't be the end of the world if prices go up. I'm not worried about not having enough money. God will give me the resources and take care of my needs.
- I don't feel compelled to hold on to things "just in case." When "just in case" happens, God will be there.

God taught me to depend on Him as He gave me the people, resources, and strength to de-junk my heart and home. With every prayer, my tight-fisted grasp to material possessions loosened. I stopped wanting more and became content with less. Through Him, I am freed from a lifestyle of too much stuff.

SOMETHING TO THINK ABOUT

- In what areas do you need to start accepting responsibility? Where can you do a better job?
- Do you need to make peace with people or events from your past? What steps can you take to begin that process today?
- What have you learned from your life's challenges? How have they helped you to grow?
- What faith issues come into play for you when you de-clutter?
- How can God free you from the too-much-stuff lifestyle?

HOMEBUILDING

Now to him who is able to do immeasurably more than all we ask or imagine, according to his power that is at work within us, to him be glory in the church and in Christ Jesus throughout all generations, for ever and ever! Amen. —Ephesians 3:20-22

When God is at work within us, let's give Him the glory. *Thank you, Lord, for transforming my heart and home. Amen.*

SMALL GROUP STUDY

Re-read the Scripture verses for each chapter.

Introduction: The Ultimate Cost of Clutter (Jeremiah 29:11).

1. Why does God love you in spite of your messes—and not just the physical ones you make in your house?
2. How does clutter impact your spiritual growth?
3. How does clutter impact your relationships?
4. What kind of future do you envision God might have for you once you de-junk your home?
5. Write a couple paragraphs on what your life would be like if your home was clear of clutter. How would you feel in the morning when you wake up to face the day? How would it change your interactions with loved ones? How would your life be different?

Chapter 1: Declaring War on Clutter (Proverbs 24:3-4)

1. What are the rare and beautiful treasures that fill your home— the kind you can't buy in a department store?
2. What makes a treasure rare and beautiful?
3. Take a look at your checkbook and your calendar. Based on what you see, what types of treasure are you are seeking? What does that say about your heart?
4. How will you work to loosen your grasp on material possessions? What will you do to free yourself from the emotional attachments to the things that can't love you back?
5. How will you invest more in people? Carefully consider your answer. Investing in working to buy more stuff for loved ones is not necessarily the same thing as investing in those relationships.

Chapter 2: Clutter Boot Camp (Romans 12:2)

1. Define the word *conform*. How does the world entice us to conform to its standards in terms of material possessions?
2. How do you stop conforming to the world?
3. Define *transform* and *renew*. How has God transformed you by renewing your mind? What new attitudes have you embraced in the last year that indicate spiritual growth? The last five years? Ten years? Twenty years?
4. How does the dictionary define the term *will*? How might clutter prevent you from living out God's will?
5. How do know God's will for your life? Can you know it? What do you use as a litmus to test to determine if something falls under God's will?

Chapter 3: Plan Your Attack (2 Corinthians 10:3-4)

1. What is the difference between a worldly battle and a spiritual battle in the clutter war?
2. What worldly weapons have you been using in your battle against too much stuff?
3. What are spiritual weapons? How can you use them to fight your desire for more things?
4. Define stronghold and addiction. In lieu of their definitions, could you be addicted to material possessions? How might they be a stronghold in your life?
5. How will you live in the world, yet battle clutter physically and spiritually?

Chapter 4: Battle of the Bulging Home (Ephesians 6:13-17)

1. Consider the armor of God: How do you stand firm with the belt of truth, the breastplate of righteousness, and your feet fitted with readiness from the Gospel?
2. How do you take up the shield of faith to protect you from arrows? What kinds of arrows attack you? How does this armor defend you?

3. What does it mean to take the helmet of Salvation and sword of the Spirit?

4. What do you do in order to dress yourself in this armor on a daily basis? How does it help attack clutter and defend from further accumulation of stuff?

5. What is your strongest peace of armor? What makes it strong? Is there a piece of armor that you feel has been weakened? What will you do strengthen it?

Chapter 5: Paper Warfare (Proverbs 3:3)

1. How does God express His love for you—through what He has done in the past and what He is doing today?

2. How do you show faithfulness in caring for what God has given you—your talents, physical possessions, the people in your life?

3. Why do love and faithfulness go together? What does it mean to bind them around your neck and write them on the tablet of your heart?

4. If you were to read what's on the tablet of your heart today, what would it say? What do you want it to say?

5. What does love and faithfulness have to do with de-cluttering your heart and home?

Chapter 6: Escape from Laundry Mountain (Matthew 6:28-30)

1. How does worry correlate with faith?

2. Do you worry about what would happen if you parted with certain items? If yes, what do you worry about and why? If no, then why do you insist on holding on to so much stuff?

3. Was there a time when you were forced to depend on God? What happened?

4. What would your life be like if you stopped keeping things because you might need them someday and simply trusted in God?

5. What small step of faith will you take today by letting go of some of your possessions?

Chapter 7: Combatting the Clutter (Philippians 4:12-13)

1. How do you define contentment? How will embracing an attitude of contentment help to keep a clean home?
2. What is the secret to contentment? What does it look like to be content in times of plenty? In times of scarcity? What does it look like to be discontent? Which one are you?
3. How does God give you strength—especially during those times when you feel too exhausted to clean or lack the motivation to de-clutter?
4. What are some of the things you are most thankful for?
5. Think of an important person in your life. Does this person know how much he or she means to you? How can you express your thankfulness for how this person has loved, encouraged, and supported you? Do something today to let that person know how you feel.

Chapter 8: The Clean Dream (James 1:2-4)

1. What are some of the trials you face in your battle to de-clutter?
2. Do you consider cleaning your home to be a joy or a misery? How can you develop a better attitude about it?
3. Why is it important to develop perseverance?
4. How does a never-give-up attitude help you mature?
5. How do we not lack in anything when we don't get everything we want?

Chapter 9: Invisible Clutter (Psalm 139:23-24)

1. What types of spiritual clutter lay hidden in your heart? How will you go about de-cluttering your heart?
2. How does physical clutter affect your relationship with God? What are its impacts on your mind and heart?

3. What burdens are you carrying today? Are you taking on other people's weights as well as your own? How would your life be different if you let go of the invisible clutter that weighs you down and let God take control of your life?

4. Do you need to recommit your life to God? If so write a prayer to Him. Ask Him to come alongside you as you deal with the messes no one but He can see.

5. Are you living without Jesus—the One with the power to de-clutter your life from the inside out? If so, invite Him into your heart.

Chapter 10: Saboteurs of a Clean Home (Proverbs 4:23)

1. Refer to your dictionary: What is the definition for *wellspring*? What is the definition for *heart*?

2. How does physical clutter plug or pollute your wellspring?

3. How will you guard your heart from invisible clutter?

4. What can you do to protect your heart from the impact of too much stuff?

5. One way to guard your heart is through rest. What are you doing to rest and recharge yourself physically, mentally, and spiritually?

Chapter 11: Money Talks, Clutter Walks (Hebrews 13:5)

1. Eliminating all credit cards is one way of placing trust in God. In what specific ways do you put your trust in the Lord?

2. What is the difference between money being the root of evil and the love of money being the root of evil?

3. What does it mean to be discontent? How do you show discontentment?

4. In what areas do you still need to learn to be content? How will you work on developing contentment in those areas?

5. Do you ever feel as if God has forsaken you? How do you know in your mind that He's at work in your life even though you might not feel it in your heart?

Chapter 12: Breaking Free (Ephesians 3:20-22)

1. When did God do something for you that was more than what you could have asked or imagined? Explain.
2. What is God doing in your life today?
3. How have the challenges of maintaining a presentable home helped you draw closer to God?
4. What does it look like to glorify God in the little things? In the big things? How are you doing that in your life? Give specific examples.
5. How often do you thank God for the blessings He pours into your life? Say a prayer of thanksgiving, naming the things you are thankful for. Remember to thank Him for being at work in your heart and home.

APPENDIX

Help for Hoarders and Clutter Warriors

As you gear up to battle the clutter in your home, you may want to check out some additional resources.

The International OCD Foundation Web site at ocfoundation.org/hoarding is where you can learn in-depth about the nuances of hoarding and how to find treatment. If you or a loved one struggle with too much stuff, the first place I recommend going for help is this premier Web site for information on hoarding. Click every link and absorb their resources.

The Institute for Challenging Disorganization, formerly the National Study Group on Chronic Disorganization, offers search capabilities to find professional organizers trained in working with clients who struggle with extreme clutter. They also provide free downloads to publications on hoarding. Visit them at challengingdisorganization.org.

The National Association of Professional Organizers (NAPO) provides assistance in finding professional organizers as well as tips on getting organized. Check out their Web site at napo.net

Faithful Organizers is an organization that connects Christian homemakers with Christian professional organizers. You can find a list of Christian professional organizers by state at faithfulorganizers.com.

Messies Anonymous offers support groups for anyone struggling with clutter. Visit messies.com to find a support group near you.

Clutterwise provides additional resources by the author on de-cluttering and getting organized. Get updates on workshop locations and information regarding online coaching at clutterwise.com.

ACKNOWLEDGMENTS

With thankfulness to God, I extend my gratitude to the many people who supported me in my de-cluttering and publishing journey.

Jan McCormick: Your wise words changed my life and the lives of many of my readers: *You can't keep everything and keep a clean house.*

Holly Tiemann: You are the best cheerleader ever!

Kim Flynn: When this book was just an idea in my head, you were my creative sounding board.

Donita K. Paul: I appreciate your gentle guidance into the publishing industry.

Thanks to my critique group from years ago. Without you, my writing would still sound like a graduate thesis: Paul Moede, Jack Hagar, Dianna Gay, Stuart Stockton, and Donita K. Paul.

To my friends Debra Canale, Susan Simpson, Linda Harris, Shanna Schutte, David Bishop, Scoti Domeij, Beth Vogt, Steven Saint-Thomas, and Liz Duckworth: With much gratitude for your editing, support, and encouragement.

To Judi Perry and the rest of the Beacon Hill team: Thank you for capturing the vision for the first edition and getting this updated edition out there.

Brandon Hill: I LOVE the cover! You have incredible talent.

Bonnie Manuella: Thanks for taking time out of your life to join me on the writing road in New Mexico.

Pamela Duffy: You have a brilliant and creative mind. You make a great content editor.

Susan Simpson: You inspire me. Enough said.

Dad: Thanks for giving your blessing to sharing our story. You are an awesome father. I'm glad you're my dad.

Owen Porter: I love your beautiful mind. You are funny, creative, and keep me on my toes. I became a writer because of you.

Troy Porter: Thank you for being our family provider so that I can be a stay-at-home mom and writer. I love you for living with less so that we can have more.

Love to all,
Kathryn

Teach Your Children to Love Like Jesus

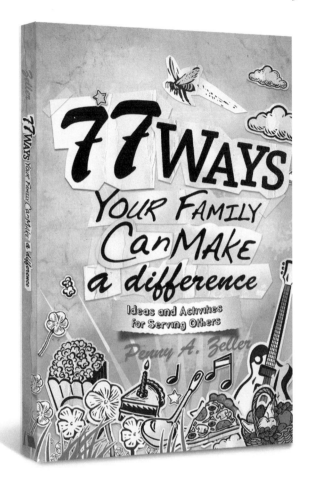

Serving others—loving them the way we love ourselves—is the heartbeat of the Christian faith. Packed with 77 suggestions and activities designed to serve the needs of people in your community, this fun and insightful book will help you cultivate love and compassion in your kids as you discover ways your family can make the world a better place by impacting the lives of others.

77 Ways Your Family Can Make a Difference
ISBN 978-0-8341-2370-0

Available wherever books are sold.
www.BeaconHillBooks.com

Where can you find the retreat you need?

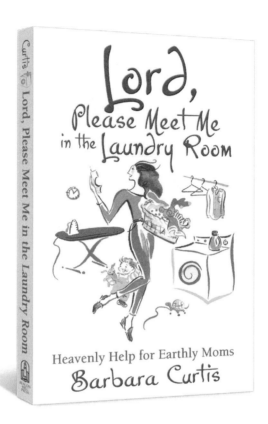

Lord, Please Meet Me in the Laundry Room brings ideas for spiritual retreats into the everyday life of busy moms. This book will unburden, enlighten, amuse, and encourage you in your hectic daily life.

Lord, Please Meet Me in the Laundry Room
By Barbara Curtis
ISBN: 978-0-8341-2097-6

Do you long to fall in love with God?

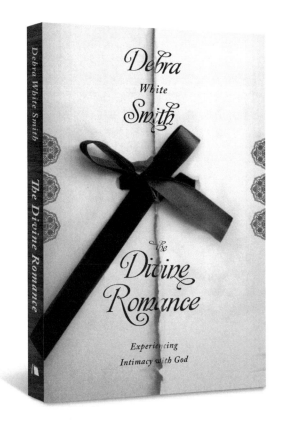

In this inspiring and relevant book, Debra White Smith shows you how to satisfy your nagging hunger for the fullness of God's love. Through the author's helpful insights and solid biblical wisdom, you will begin the journey of a deepening romance with the Lord that will bring you ever nearer to the heart of God.

THE DIVINE ROMANCE
By Debra White Smith
ISBN: 978-0-8341-2443-1

BEACON HILL PRESS
OF KANSAS CITY

Available online and wherever books are sold.